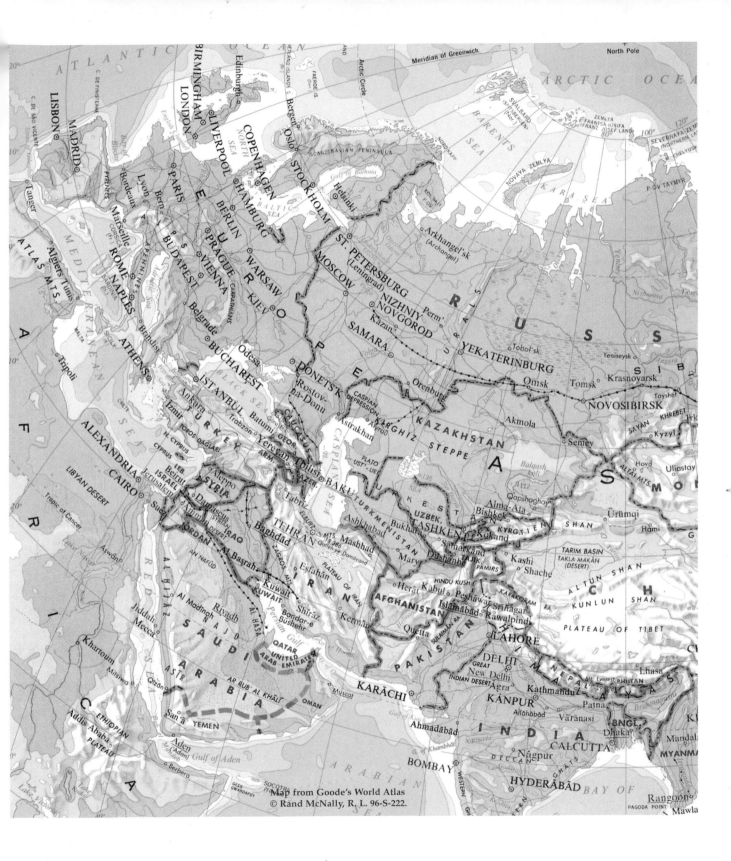

Map from Goode's World Atlas
© Rand McNally, R. L. 96-S-222.

Map from Cosmopolitan World Atlas © Rand McNally, R. L. 96-S-222.

Enchantment of the World

TURKEY

By Luis A. Baralt

Consultant for Turkey: Nancy Leinwand, Ph.D., American Research
Institute in Turkey, Philadelphia, Pennsylvania

CHILDREN'S PRESS®
A Division of Grolier Publishing
New York • London • Hong Kong • Sydney
Danbury, Connecticut

A father and his sons fish on the Dalyan River.

Project Editor and Design:
Jean Blashfield Black

Library of Congress
Cataloging-in-Publication Data

Baralt, Luis A.
Turkey / by Luis A. Baralt.
    p. cm. -- (Enchantment of the world)
Includes index.
    Summary: Examines the geography, history, economy, people, and culture of Turkey, which stands at the hub of Asia, Africa, and Europe.
    ISBN 0-516-20305-3
    1. Turkey—Juvenile literature. [1. Turkey.] I. Title. II. Series.
    DR417.B37 1997
    915.61—dc21   96-49594
                                                            CIP
                                                            AC

Photo credits ©: Aramco World: 20 left; Art Resource: 14 bottom, 36 top (Giraudon), 13, 29 left, 30 top (Erich Lessing), 9 bottom (Scala); Asia Access: 46, 77 top, 80, 100, 101, 108 inset, 109, 110 top (Jeffrey Alford), 11 left, 18 top, 87, 105 (Naomi Duguid); Comstock: 4, 40 top, 90 (Henry Georgi), 5, 65; Corbis-Bettmann: 16 top, 21 top, 22 top, 23, 34, 35, 36 bottom, 37, 42, 70, 73, 84; Folio, Inc.: 17, 20 right (Rob Crandall), 83 right (Hameed Gorani), 89 (Richard Quataert), 63, 91 (Catherine Ursillo); Impact Visuals: 43 inset, 58 right (Olivia Heussler), 111 (Axel Koster); John Elk III: 9 top, 14 top, 30 inset, 54 bottom, 77 inset, 78 left, 94, 102; Magnum Photos: 56 left, 68 (Abbas), 57 (Bruno Barbey), 50 left, 62 right, 97, 107, 110 inset (Ara Guler), 54 top, 56 right, 61 left (Richard Kalvar); Mary Altier: 40 bottom, 47, 50 right, 52 bottom left, 58 left, 61 right, 67 right, 92 bottom, 99 left, 104; Nik Wheeler: 45, 108 top; North Wind Picture Archives: 10, 18 bottom, 22 bottom; Photri: 6, 29 right (Richard T. Nowitz), 8, 25 left, 25 right, 26, 41, 78 right; Superstock, Inc.: cover, 52 center, 52 bottom right, 59, 62 left, 92 top, 94 left, 96 left; Tony Stone Images: 12, 49 right, 103 (Robert Frerck), 67 left, 96 right (Gary Yeowell); United Nations: 43 top; UPI/Corbis-Bettmann: 38, 60; Wolfgang Kaehler: 21 inset, 11 right, 16 inset, 19, 27, 32, 33, 52 top, 74, 75, 82, 83 left, 85, 86, 88, 99 right.

Cover photo: The Red Tower in Alanya

This family in Cappadocia travels to market by horse and wagon.

TABLE OF CONTENTS

Chapter 1   *Hub and Legend* (The Land, The Fountainhead, Seljuks and Ottomans) 7

Chapter 2   *Istanbul: Bridge Over the Ages* (The Setting, Dawn of Three Millennia, The Christian Millennium) 15

Chapter 3   *Days of the Crescent* (Centuries of the Ottomans, Suleyman the Lawgiver, Decline and Rebirth, Ataturk) 31

Chapter 4   *Today's Turkey* (Rebuilding the Nation, Government, Economy, Agriculture and Other Resources, Mining and Industry, Services) 39

Chapter 5   *Everyday Life* (What is a Turk?, Population Growth, Women and the Turkish Family, Youth and Sports, Education, Foods of Turkey) 55

Chapter 6   *Islam —The Religious Life* (Last Prophet, Seeds of Division, Spread of Islam, Faith of Islam, The Five Pillars) 69

Chapter 7   *The Cultural Scene* (Architecture, Literature and Performing Arts, Plastic Arts and Museums, Carpet Weaving and More) 81

Chapter 8   *Cities and Places* (Ankara, Izmir, Adana, Antakya and the Turkish Riviera, Black Sea Coastline, Central Anatolia, Eastern Anatolia, The Future) 93

Mini-Facts at a Glance 113

Index 123

The city walls of Alanya keep the town from tumbling down the rugged cliffs into the Aegean Sea.

Chapter 1

HUB AND LEGEND

Two facts stand out when we study Turkey. First is its central position at the hub of three continents, where Asia, Africa, and Europe are closest to each other. Second is the great antiquity (more than three thousand years) of its recorded history.

The first fact accounts for the diversity of Turkey's people and their cultural values and traditions. The second explains the Turkish nation's deep sense of pride and heritage.

THE LAND

Turkey's land mass is unevenly divided between Europe and Asia. The country occupies 301,382 square miles (780,576 square kilometers)—about the size of Texas and Oklahoma combined. Only about 3 percent of the country is in Europe, occupying the southeastern tip of the Balkan Peninsula. The rest occupies the entire Anatolian Peninsula of Asia, part of what is sometimes called Asia Minor. Anatolia juts out into the Mediterranean Sea, making it a crossroads of migration and invasion routes between the three continents throughout the ages.

The sources of the Tigris and Euphrates Rivers are located at the eastern base of the Anatolian Peninsula. To the south, between the banks of these rivers in present-day Iraq, the early civilizations of Sumer and Akkad arose. Later states and cities of the

This photo taken by a satellite shows the Tigris and Euphrates Rivers in Iraq. The oldest known Western civilizations developed between these two rivers, both of which arise in the mountains of eastern Turkey.

Mesopotamian plain included Assyria, Babylonia, Nineveh, and Ur.

Three-quarters of Turkey's borders are on water. The Black Sea is on the north and the Mediterranean and Aegean Seas are on the southwest and west. The countries that border Turkey are Greece and Bulgaria on the west, Syria and Iraq on the south, Iran and Armenia on the east, and Georgia on the north. Both Armenia and Georgia were part of the former Soviet Union.

Turkey's varied topography includes rugged mountain ranges in the west and south, high plateaus in the central areas, and, in the east, a mixture of fertile river plains and lake country, accented by more towering mountain ranges. Individual peaks rise to great heights. The Bible says that Noah's Ark landed on Mount Ararat, which is 17,011 feet (5,185 meters) high.

Turkey lies wholly in the temperate zone. Istanbul, the largest

Mount Ararat is in eastern Turkey near the Iran border.

city, is about the same latitude as New York City and Naples, Italy. However, western Turkey's climate is moderated by the Mediterranean Sea. The central and eastern plateaus and mountainous areas are subject to more extreme temperatures.

THE FOUNTAINHEAD

The Turkic peoples, also called Turks, had their origins in central Asia. (Note that the word "Turkish," ending in "sh," not

The Lion Gate was built by the Hittites, probably the first civilization to arise in Turkey.

The Huns, nomadic people from Mongolia, under the leadership of Attila, invaded Asia Minor, leaving Turkic peoples to settle the area.

"c," is reserved for the citizens of the modern state.) They were an offshoot of the Huns, about whom solid records exist from the eighth century B.C. The Huns, originally pastoral nomads from Mongolia, had spread through the centuries, by steady migratory currents and warlike invasions, into western Asia and Europe. One of their renowned leaders was Attila, who in the fifth century A.D. conquered the Balkan Peninsula, invaded France and Spain, and laid siege to Rome. The Turkic tribes eventually became the primary people in Turkmenistan, Tajikistan, Azerbaijan, Uzbekistan, and, of course, Turkey.

At the beginning, there were many separate tribes among the Turkic peoples. Various tribes reached their greatest strength in different regions of central Asia, developing different cultures, though at a primitive level. But, after the eighth century A.D., the various tribes all came into contact with Islam, the religion of Muhammad. This contact tended to unify the tribes, letting them develop a common language and culture.

Turkic cities such as Bukhara and Samarkand in central Asia became wealthy trade hubs and centers of knowledge. Schools,

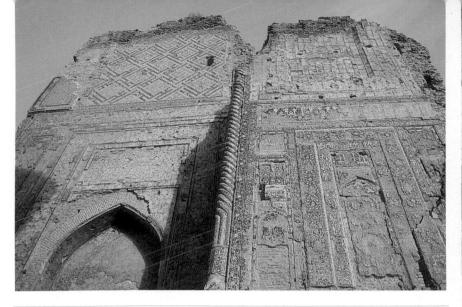

Turkic peoples settled Uzbekistan, where the ruins of a caravansery shown above are found. The woman at the right is an Uzbek living in Samarkand.

impressive mosques (Islamic houses of worship), bridges, and caravanseries were built, and many still stand. The caravanseries were often great palace inns where the caravans of trader-travelers stopped for the night and the people exchanged information. These were the first motels.

THE SELJUKS AND OTTOMANS

During the eleventh century A.D., one dominant Turkic tribe, the Oguz, succeeded in unifying many other tribes. The Oguz rulers, descendants of one leader named Seljuk, established the so-called Seljuk Empire. The Seljuks conquered a good part of western Asia, including most of the Anatolian Peninsula. The rest of Anatolia remained for a while longer under the control of the Byzantine Empire, also called the Eastern Roman Empire. The Byzantine Empire included parts of three regions: southern and

*The remains of a Seljuk seaport at Alanya overlook one of Turkey's
many beautiful beaches.*

eastern Europe, northern Africa, and the Middle East.

In the centuries that followed, regions and cities under the
Seljuk Turks prospered. They absorbed the cultural influences of
the declining Byzantines in Constantinople, which is present-day
Istanbul, as well as of the sophisticated, but also declining,
Persians to the south and east. The Persians, originally from the
area of present-day Iran, established medical schools and
theological centers, where religious thought and philosophical
studies were undertaken.

The unity did not last, however. The strong Seljuk Empire was
gradually replaced by a patchwork of rival principalities. This
development delayed the next wave of Turkic expansion for a
couple of hundred years.

By the fourteenth century, one of the principalities, that of the

Ottoman Turks, became prominent. It benefited from being located by the borders of the Byzantine Empire and its continued willingness to fight both kin and foe in neighboring Anatolia. It became the strongest state in the Islamic group of nations. And then in 1453, under Sultan (king) Fatih Mehmet II, the Ottomans conquered Constantinople. In taking Constantinople, the Ottomans took over one of the most powerful empires the world had ever seen. They then built it into an even vaster empire. Eventually that empire became the much smaller, but stable and modern republic that is today's Turkey.

Sultan Fatih Mehmet II, also known as Mohammed II, captured the city of Constantinople in 1453 and made it the capital of his empire. He was afterwards known as Mehmet the Conqueror.

The surrounding waters play a role in the life of almost every resident of modern Istanbul (above). Even the earliest maps, such as this sixteenth-century mariner's map (below), showed the straits and seas.

Chapter 2

ISTANBUL: BRIDGE OVER THE AGES

There are many cities well known for occupying entire islands (Venice, Stockholm, and New York) or bridging the shores of great rivers (Budapest on the Danube). But there is only one city—Istanbul—that occupies parts of two continents (Europe and Asia). The modern nation of Turkey, of course, does the same. But in the case of Istanbul, which is on the banks of the strait called the Bosporus, this physical feature may be symbolic of more important characteristics. Istanbul offers infinite variety and complexity. Both ancient and modern, it is considered one of the world's major melting pots of races and cultures.

In fact, when America's great "melting pot," New York City, was nothing more than a modest Dutch trading post, Istanbul was a thriving metropolis with well over two thousand years of history, though under other names, behind it. It had been the capital city of the earth's most powerful empire (Rome) and, as such, capital of the civilized world. It had become the seat of the no-less-powerful Ottoman Empire. It boasted the largest and mightiest fortifications in Eurasia. It also was the acknowledged meeting point of the races and religions of two continents.

All of these titles were deserved. And today, modern Istanbul

The Old City of Istanbul (above) lies in Europe, while just across the Bosporus lies Asia, which can be visited without leaving the city.

embodies the added reflected glory of more recent centuries of history. It particularly bears the imprint of the decades since Mustafa Kemal, called "Ataturk," launched his modernizing revolution and created the Turkish Republic. This event brought the country into the society of Western nations. It also left the mix of old and new, of tradition and renovation, that makes Istanbul so amazing in the eye of the first-time visitor.

Today Istanbul (some believe the name to be derived from *Islambol*, meaning "the city of Islam") is a huge metropolis of countless palaces, museums, mosques, churches, and monuments. It is a noisy, bustling place. The pursuit of money, pleasure, and

The Sea of Marmara is seen here looking past the Sultanahmet Mosque.

power coexists with quieter, but no less earnest, strivings in religious matters. Although no longer the capital, Istanbul is the center of much of Turkey's cultural life.

THE SETTING

A map of the great land masses of Eurasia and Africa, such as that shown on the first page of this book, shows two large bodies of water that mark clear limits between Europe proper and the countries of southwestern Asia or northern Africa. These are the Black Sea and the Mediterranean Sea. There also is a connection between these two great seas—a smaller body of water called the Sea of Marmara. This small sea is completely surrounded by Turkish territory, but it also divides the continents of Europe and Asia. The Sea of Marmara, in turn, connects with the waters of the Aegean Sea, really a bay of the Mediterranean, through a channel or strait

The minarets, or towers, of mosques and a lighted ocean navigation buoy
stand out against the sunset over the Golden Horn.

called the Dardanelles. And it is also connected to the Black Sea
through another strait, the Bosporus. It is on the shores of the
Bosporus and an elongated inlet piercing the European Peninsula,
known as the Golden Horn, that sprawling Istanbul is situated.

The whole area where Istanbul is located is wrapped in a
confusing mix of myth and fact. In Greek mythology, Jason and his
Argonauts sailed through the Bosporus in search of the Golden
Fleece. In historical fact, these waterways have, from the beginnings
of recorded history, served as migration or invasion
routes for the peoples of each continent.

Early in the fifth century B.C., King
Darius of Persia fought the Scythians,
campaigned into what is now Russia,

Jason and other demigods and heroes of Greek
myth sailed the ship Argo from the Aegean Sea,
through the Bosporus, and into the Black Sea in
their search for the Golden Fleece.

18

The Grand Bazaar is in Stamboul, the old heart of the city.

and sent his fleets to secure the shores of the Black Sea to the east and capture Greek islands on the Aegean to the west. And his son, Xerxes, spanned the Hellespont (another name for the Dardanelles) with a floating bridge, then marched a huge invasion force across it with the ill-fated intent of conquering the Greek city-states. Two centuries later, Alexander the Great used these same waterways to ship his armies into Asia and conquer the Persian Empire.

The Bosporus is some 20 miles (32 kilometers) long. Its hilly abrupt shores are scattered with castles and sumptuous villas—remnants of its rich past—as well as the more modern, sprawling beach resorts that cater to leisure-seeking citizens of Istanbul.

Istanbul is divided by these waterways into three main areas or districts. On the European side of the Bosporus, southern shore of the Golden Horn, and northern shore of the Sea of Marmara, lies Stamboul, the antique core of the city. This district abounds in old

A modern bridge across the Bosporus (left) takes people to the Beyoglu, or New City (above). It is a crowded section of office and apartment buildings built on a slope going down toward the water.

palaces, Islamic places of worship called mosques, and markets, or bazaars, within a mesh of steamy old streets and alleys.

To the north of the Golden Horn and connected to Stamboul through the Galata Bridge (which takes its name from the old tower located at its northern end), lies Beyoglu, the relatively more modern section. Beyoglu, with its myriad office buildings, shops, and aging tenements, slopes busily southwest toward the waters of the Golden Horn. But at its eastern and northern confines, Beyoglu opens up into modern suburbs, parks, and luxury hotels.

The third district—Uskudar—lies across the straits in Asia. It is connected to Beyoglu by two single-span hanging bridges built in modern times, the last one finished as recently as 1988. Uskudar is a sprawling sector of growing industry and modern housing, and it enjoys increasing importance today because of its closeness to

Uskudar (above) is the Asiatic portion
of Istanbul, which can be reached by
boat or over bridges. Clearly, water is
vital to Istanbul's life. Fishermen
(right) can carry on their work within
sight of the city's heart.

the land route connecting Istanbul with Ankara, Turkey's capital
since the founding of the republic.

Water, then, is the vital fluid in which the city delights. From
any one of its vantage points—hilltops, towers, bridges—an
observer can easily appreciate the importance to the city of its
waterways. And within its small streets and alleys water is equally
present in the form of winter mists and summer steaminess.

DAWN OF THREE MILLENNIA

The name *Istanbul* is the third by which the city has been
known. It was previously called *Byzantium* and*Constantinople*.
Scholars are not certain about the actual birth of the city. There is

Homer, the Greek poet, told stories of ancient Troy, near Istanbul, which are still enjoyed today.

evidence that numerous settlements established along the shores of the Bosporus and the adjacent waterways can be traced back to remote prehistoric times. For instance, the famous mound of Hisarlik, which is located near the city on the Anatolian Peninsula, is believed to be the site of the fabled Troy—a city made famous by the Greek poet Homer and the Roman poet Virgil. Excavations at the site have revealed the existence of at least eight other layers of cities, the oldest one dating back to perhaps 3000 years B.C., while fabled Troy itself may date from approximately 1300 B.C.

It is likely that by the eighth century B.C. there was a Greek settlement located on or near the present site of Uskudar, which was already a strategic crossroads between the two land masses. Two centuries later, legend has it, pioneering Greek travelers led by a man named Byzas were tipped off by the Oracle of Delphi (an oracle is a prophet with special powers) as to the existence of an even better strategic site in the area. Following instructions from the Oracle, Byzas and his companions proceeded to found the little town of Byzantium on the European side of the strait.

Through the following centuries, the

Philip of Macedonia besieged Byzantium, which resisted the attack.

In his quest to replenish the treasury of Macedonia, Alexander the Great, shown with his great horse, Bucephalus, attacked and captured Byzantium.

residents of Byzantium were Greeks. The small city was seen as an important prize of war by the Persians and the Greek city-states of Athens and Sparta. It changed hands a number of times and ultimately fell to warriors from the country of Macedonia north of Greece. Byzantium's reputation grew when it managed heroically to resist the siege of Philip of Macedonia. Yet a few years later, Byzantium yielded readily to Philip's son, Alexander the Great. However, it regained its independence when Alexander's empire crumbled after his death.

As a free city, Byzantium grew in importance and wealth. It managed to fight off the occasional invasions of barbarians from the north. But it slowly found itself increasingly under the control of imperial Rome. At the end of the second century A.D., the city sided with a faction that tried to revolt against the Roman Empire. As a penalty, the Roman emperor Septimus Severus razed Byzantium and massacred its inhabitants. A few years later, he rebuilt it on a much grander scale as a tribute to his victories. The new Byzantium was sacked in 268 by another Roman emperor on the rampage, Gallienus. Then the city grew and became a truly unassailable fortress. It withstood further invasions and remained unharmed through civil wars and rebellions.

The great Rome itself was already under attack from outside raiders. It also had begun to decline as an empire from the inside. By the latter part of the third century A.D., the Roman Empire had been split into four parts—Gaul and Britain, the Danubian countries, Italy and Africa, and the East. The Roman emperor Diocletian, struggling to reorganize a waning empire, created a shared rule by four emperors—two Augusti and two Caesars, with himself as an Augustus. The measure had its merit, but in a few years the system dissolved in turmoil and strife.

The heir to one of Diocletian's four subempires was Constantine, whose administrative talent gradually placed him over the other emperors. In the year 324, he defeated the last of his enemies at a site near Byzantium and became head of the whole Roman Empire. Within weeks of Constantine's victory, he proclaimed Byzantium to be the new Rome. He renamed the city Constantinople, "City of Constantine," and started building the foundations of a much-enlarged capital city. On May 11, 330, the city of Constantinople was officially inaugurated.

THE CHRISTIAN MILLENNIUM

Before Constantine, Byzantium was already a great urban center and an important city fortress. It also enjoyed a reputation as a haven for peoples of different cultural and racial backgrounds. But its selection as capital of a great empire by an equally great emperor became an act of enormous historical significance. Constantine was not only a great leader and soldier, but a

Above: The town of Seljuk contains the remains of a Roman aqueduct.
Right: After seeing the Cross in the sky, and with the encouragement of his mother, Constantine converted to Christianity. Twelve years later, he was declared the new emperor and turned Byzantium into his new capital, Constantinople.

thoughtful administrator and a conscientious, inspired innovator in matters of faith. Influenced by his mother, who was later known as Saint Helena, Constantine had converted to Christianity. He stopped the persecutions of Christians, which had fearfully increased during Diocletian's reign, and proclaimed total freedom of religious belief in his city. But, predictably, he favored his own faith, and he endowed Constantinople with magnificent churches.

In its new status, Byzantium/Constantinople became capital of the Roman Empire, which made it the capital of the known civilized world. Rome itself was dropped temporarily to secondary rank in most matters. Constantinople grew in wealth and riches. It became a metropolis peopled mainly by Greeks, ruled under Roman law, and worshiping in the Christian faith. The people spoke Latin and classical and popular Greek, as well as many other languages. In a cultural sense, Constantinople brought about a fusion of taste and

The ancient Hippodrome, seen at left front, was a center for horse races.

tradition of both the Western and the Eastern customs, principally in art and architecture.

The city walls that Constantine put up for his new capital tripled the area of the existing city. Within those walls, he erected vast imperial structures. He built a grandiose Hippodrome (a stadium for horse and chariot races), as well as an enormous palace, legislative halls, statues and monuments, and, most of all, great churches. The church called Santa Sophia, now the present-day museum known to the Turks as *Hagia Sophia*, meaning "Divine Wisdom," was first erected by Constantine in 325. Santa Sophia boasts what many art historians consider one of the architectural marvels of all time—its beautiful 105-foot (32-meter)-wide dome. The great church was damaged by fires and an earthquake several times. But it was always rebuilt, and the sixth century's reconstruction by Emperor Justinian still stands.

Hagia Sophia is a Byzantine church (now a museum) in Istanbul that was built in the fourth century. A thousand years later, when it was turned into an Islamic mosque, the four minarets, or towers, were added.

During that first century of its new status, Constantinople's wealth and population continued to grow. John Chrysostom, a writer and priest of the period, tells of many nobles possessing from ten to twenty mansions within the city and owning as many as two thousand slaves. No wonder Constantine's original walls became too confining. The need for safety from the "barbarians" (a word more closely meaning "outlanders" than "savages") led to the building of new defensive walls. Those erected by Emperor Theodosius II in the early fifth century are the walls standing today, though the city has long since sprawled past them.

By the year 530, at the beginning of Emperor Justinian's reign, Constantinople had a population of more than half a million and had reached its heyday. It suffered through fires, a repression, and a terrible plague, but the great and wise Justinian did much to rebuild. He also added new buildings, such as the church of Saints Sergius and Bacchus, known today as the mosque of *Kucuk Ayasofya,* meaning "Little Saint Sophie."

But after the Great Plague, during which the city lost three out of five of its inhabitants, Constantinople declined. It was frequently besieged by armies from neighboring kingdoms or barbarian tribes on the rise—Persians, Arabs on multiple occasions, Bulgars, Russians, and early offshoots of the Turkic line that was later to produce the Ottomans. But none of these succeeded in breaching Constantinople's formidable defenses.

The dubious honor of capturing the great city fell to other Christians. For centuries, Rome and Constantinople had been drifting apart. Loyal to its tradition of hospitality to all peoples, Constantinople had allowed many traders from Genoa and other Italian cities to establish themselves. And this simple fact became a source of great trouble. By the end of the twelfth century, the Italians had managed to entrench themselves into the commercial power structure of the empire and enjoyed a virtual stranglehold on its economic life. Hatred of the Italians grew, culminating in their massacre. Those who survived were forbidden to undertake any further commercial activities.

In 1204 armies of the Fourth Crusade, made up substantially of Italians, were on their way to Jerusalem. Conveniently forgetting their Holy Land objective, the crusaders took advantage of an imperial power struggle to obtain the pope's blessing for an attack on Constantinople. After a siege of several months, the crusaders managed to enter the city. They robbed and massacred the

Crusaders from western Europe captured Constantinople in 1204, as shown in the painting above by Delacroix. The remains of many crusader castles, such as that shown at the right, can still be found in Turkey.

residents, and they installed one of their own crusading knights—Baldwin of Flanders—on the throne. The pillage went on for years, and Constantinople never suffered more than throughout the fifty-seven years of the crusaders' rule. Finally, in 1261, Michael VIII Paleologus, a Greek emperor, retook the city.

The Byzantine Empire shrank as the robberies of crusaders and attacks on it by Arabs and Turks continued. Constantinople, its capital, led a precarious existence for the next two centuries. Its Galata sector across the Golden Horn (today's Beyoglu) had been granted by Michael to the Genoese as a peace offering, and it was the only sector to prosper, mostly from foreign trade. Constantinople proper, however, fell slowly into ruin and decay. To compound matters, the rising Ottoman Turks were growing strong enough to lay siege to the great city. They once more failed to take it, but by the middle of the fifteenth century, they were unstoppable. They crossed into Europe, surrounding the weakened empire.

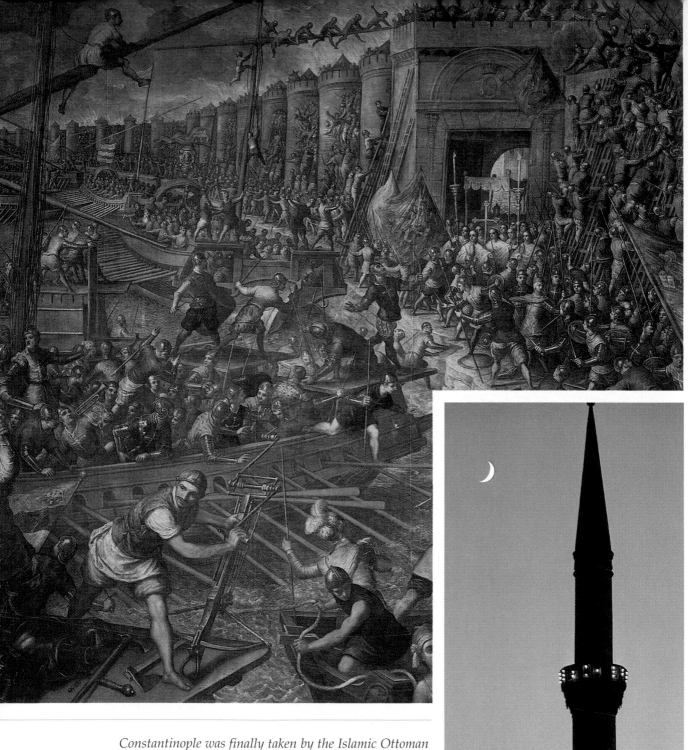

Constantinople was finally taken by the Islamic Ottoman
Turks in 1453 (above). The crescent moon (seen at right past
a minaret) became the symbol of Turkey.

Chapter 3

DAYS OF
THE CRESCENT

The 1,129 years of the Byzantine Empire, or the Eastern Roman Empire as it is also known in history, came to an end in 1453. The previous year, the Ottoman sultan, Mehmet II, had blockaded the Bosporus and erected fortifications at a narrowing of the strait. In preparing his strategy, he also ordered a set of gigantic cannon. Armed with this new artillery and a force of vastly greater numbers than the city's defenders, Mehmet laid siege to Constantinople.

The resourceful sultan even managed to outflank the city's defenses, which included an unbreakable chain across the mouth of the Golden Horn, an inlet of the Bosporus. Mehmet had his ships hauled overland around the chain into the Golden Horn. Still, Constantinople resisted heroically for nearly two months, thanks to the valor of its Genoese defenders and its fortifications.

Tradition has it that the night of May 28, 1453, was filled with omens. The moon was eclipsed and a pea-soup fog blotted out every feature of the city. At one point during that night, however, the fog parted briefly and a crescent moon shone clearly. The next day, Constantinople fell to the Turks. The reigning Byzantine emperor, Constantine XI Paleologus, was killed in battle. Mehmet decreed that his men could pillage and massacre for three days,

Over the centuries, Topkapi Palace was the home of thousands of women in the harem, or seraglio, of the Ottoman emperors.

which took care of the few remaining inhabitants of the city. The crescent moon became the symbol of the Ottoman Turks.

CENTURIES OF THE OTTOMANS

The Ottoman conquest brought peace and stability to the embattled city. Within a short while, Sultan Mehmet, undoubtedly impressed by the remnants of its former magnificence, made Constantinople his new capital. He renamed it *Istanbul* and began to repopulate it and reconstruct its buildings. Mehmet mostly brought people from the surrounding conquered Greek territories of the Peloponnese, Salonika, and the Aegean islands. But little by little, other immigrants from Anatolia and from traditionally Turkic areas drifted into the city. By the end of the fifteenth century, Istanbul's population had risen again to close to 100,000.

Mehmet, a young and forceful Muslim leader, converted the

The inside of the seraglio of Topkapi Palace was very ornate. This is the lounge where the many women spent their leisure time. Today Topkapi Palace is a museum.

great Byzantine Christian churches into Islamic mosques. But as a canny administrator, he realized that he needed the cooperation of the Christians, so he allowed them to congregate peacefully in certain churches. He also built grandiose new mosques, such as the huge Fatih Mosque and the first Eyup Mosque (which was destroyed and rebuilt several times) at the head of the Golden Horn, as well as fabulous court buildings, including Topkapi Palace. Topkapi was first intended as an austere royal residence. But later, and by other emperors, it was turned over to the sultan's *seraglio,* or "harem," which at its heyday may have included two thousand women and hundreds of eunuchs (men with their testicles removed so they could not father children).

The next hundred years of Istanbul's life was marked by a succession of relatively harmless sultans who dedicated their best efforts to beautifying the city according to their standards. Fountains, mosques, palaces, and the use of decorations inspired by nature multiplied. Statues of the human form were pulled down because such things were against Islam. Magnificent Christian art was destroyed or hidden under new facades. Some priceless Christian mosaics were painted over and thus preserved.

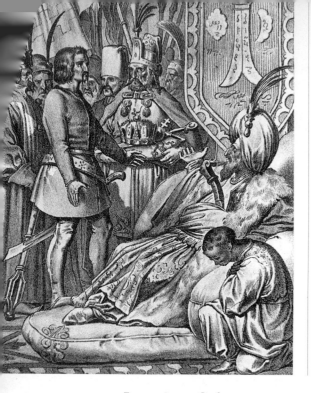

Suleyman the Magnificent's empire was so large that he could control many other kings. Here he is seen declaring a Hungarian the king of his country.

SULEYMAN THE LAWGIVER

This period reached its crowning golden era during the reign of the Ottoman sultan Suleyman the Magnificent, also known as the Lawgiver. Suleyman was a particularly wise ruler whose empire stretched from Morocco in North Africa to Afghanistan in Asia, east of Turkey, and from the shores of the Indian Ocean to Hungary in Central Europe. Suleyman was undoubtedly one of the most powerful monarchs of his day, a match to such Western counterparts as Charles V, who was both king of Spain and emperor of the Holy Roman Empire. Suleyman reorganized his empire and Istanbul along almost liberal lines. He went as far as institutionalizing freedom of worship and the rule of law. He promoted tolerance and understanding—something almost unheard of in the Europe of his time.

Suleyman, who reigned between 1520 and 1566, started the construction of magnificent buildings in the city. During the half century of his rule, he kept tight reign on the high officials, the top eunuchs, and the Janissaries. The Janissaries had been started as an elite corps of "new soldiers" recruited from the young men of conquered Christian territories. They acquired both good and bad

This detail from a sixteenth-century miniature painting shows the great sultan, Suleyman, hunting.

reputations, for their great prowess as well as ruthlessness in battle. Through the centuries, they developed into a political faction busy amassing wealth and privileges, regarding it as their right to depose or enthrone sultans. But Suleyman kept them under control.

Yet absolute power, however enlightened, carries the seed of its own destruction. Suleyman himself made the mistake of housing part of the royal harem right at the center of the affairs of state, the Topkapi Palace, while the rest remained in its relatively removed traditional location. This move had the effect of promoting intrigues and courtly tactics that ended tragically. In 1561 Suleyman took sides in the conflict over succession rights among his sons. Under the influence of the mother of one of them, a beloved younger concubine from his seraglio, Suleyman had the eldest and ablest of his sons executed. Five years later, and after further jockeying for power among the sultan's remaining sons, Suleyman's death brought about the enthronement of possibly the worst of them all, the useless Selim II, also known as the "Sot," meaning the "Drunkard."

Ottoman emperor Selim II, known to history as the "Sot," is shown holding a bow in this miniature painted about 1570.

DECLINE AND REBIRTH

Selim's reign inaugurated a series of mostly weak and vice-ridden sultanates resulting in the decline of the empire. Not until the beginning of the nineteenth century did reaction set in among the powerful people. Then, faced with the breakup of the empire, some concerned groups brought the reform-minded Mahmoud II to the throne. This sultan moved the empire into a more modern age. Mahmoud was moved by the principles of scientific advancement and parliamentary rule of law that inspired the Western nations of Europe. However, the violent opposition of the conservatives, among them the Janissaries, led to trouble. In 1826 the Janissaries' plotting leaders were massacred in the Hippodrome. This marked the end of an era and the start of Westernization for Istanbul.

Soon, direct steamship service between western Europe and Istanbul was started.

Sultan Mahmoud II, who put the Janissaries out of business

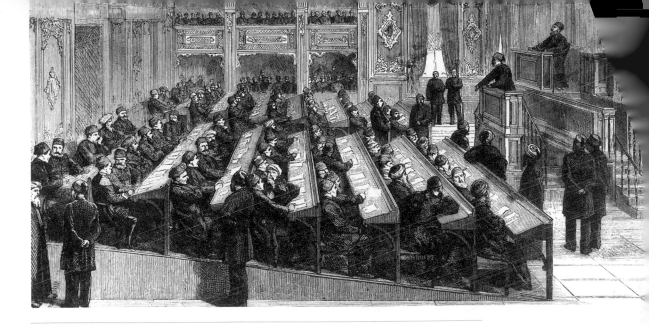

In 1876, Sultan Abdul Hamid II was persuaded by reformers to accept the first Ottoman constitution and call a parliament. His reluctance to give up power led to a brief losing war with Russia and the loss of various European territories.

The first permanent bridge over the Golden Horn was completed. In 1839 Sultan Abdulmecid I issued an edict assuring rights to all, regardless of religion. In the latter part of the century, the first railroad line connecting Istanbul with western Europe, the famous *Orient Express*, was completed, and a sophisticated water-supply system for the city and its suburbs was installed.

ATATURK

In the early part of the twentieth century, new disruptions took place in the city. These were brought about by the Ottomans' continued failures in foreign relations and the rising dissatisfaction of the younger army officers. In 1908 the Young Turk Movement, made up of educated military officers and other young men, deposed the sultan. More trouble came when Turkey sided in World War I with Germany and the other Central Powers. Istanbul

Mustafa Kemal, later known as Kemal Ataturk, became the "Father of Modern Turkey" by establishing the republic when it succeeded in winning a war against Greece after World War I. Ataturk continued to lead the nation until his death in 1938.

suffered a long-lasting and distressing blockade by Britain, France, and the other Allies. It was then occupied by Allied forces.

After the war, the discredited Ottoman government was supported by the Allied troops that remained in Turkey. The War of Independence was fought, led by the nationalistic and forward-looking Mustafa Kemal, who would later be called *Ataturk,* a word that means "Father of the Turks," because the war led to Turkey being proclaimed a republic in 1923. The capital was moved to Ankara, leaving Istanbul just a big city with no official distinction.

Ataturk moved the capital out of Istanbul in the hope of removing the political and decision-making center of the nation from the religious leaders and institutions concentrated in Istanbul. An added benefit was that the capital was no longer in proximity to Turkey's European borders, which could easily be crossed by invaders. Istanbul's character has continued to be more Westernized, though it has never lost the deep mystery and enchantment of its past.

Chapter 4

TODAY'S TURKEY

There is an old Turkish proverb, "When the wolf ages, he becomes the plaything of the dogs." This is quite fitting to describe the events the Turkish people had to face in the early part of the twentieth century. During World War I, the Ottoman Empire had joined the Central Powers—Germany, Austria-Hungary, and Bulgaria—in the alliance that pitted them against the Western Allies—the United States, England, France, Italy, Greece, etc. This was a fateful decision that brought Turkey total defeat by 1918. The economy was in a shambles, and the country was occupied by Greece, according to the terms of surrender. All the ills and failings accumulated through the declining stages of the Ottoman Empire had come to roost at one moment in history.

Many young people, as well as their older and thoughtful mentors, saw that an opportunity was open to them. Thus began a hard-fought War of Independence, which was won with Turkey's victory over Greece in 1922. All occupying forces withdrew.

REBUILDING THE NATION

In 1923 a republic was proclaimed. The next year, the caliphate, or religious monarchy, was abolished and a new constitution was

Above: A shipyard near Bodrum builds gulets, or Turkish wood-hulled yachts.
Below: A spice market in Istanbul features many herbs used in Turkish cooking.

Large banners showing Kemal Ataturk, known as the "Father of Modern Turkey," continue to be shown on special occasions, many decades after his death.

adopted. Behind these developments stood the Young Turk Movement. Its unquestioned leader was Mustafa Kemal, later known as Ataturk, a prestigious soldier and hero. But Ataturk was more than just a hero. He was a forward-thinking, inventive, cultured man. He realized that if his nation were to survive in a modern world, it would do so only by modernizing.

Ataturk and his confederates stood for nationalism and security from the nation's enemies beyond its borders. This was in accordance with a traditional and universal creed. But they also stood for other, more surprising values. Some of these they pressed on with immediately. Others, promoted by elite leaders such as Ismet Inonu, a friend and follower of Ataturk's, took some time in materializing. Ataturk and his followers came to believe, for instance, in egalitarianism (equal rights for all citizens under the law), and in freedom of faith (Christians as well as all other minorities were to be guaranteed the same rights as Muslims). They also stood for the principles of reform. They believed that the state could evolve and change through experience instead of stagnating in adopted forms.

Ismet Inonu, one of the "Young Turks," was the first prime minister of the new Turkish Republic. He served as president after the death of Kemal Ataturk.

Ataturk renounced one-man rule and adopted democracy, although he himself came to lead the nation somewhat like a benevolent dictator. Ataturk believed in international cooperation and in solving problems through peaceful means, while keeping up the country's defenses.

After Ataturk's death in 1938, difficult times lay ahead. Those who felt they were the inheritors of his truths bickered, broke up, and threatened at times to cast his heritage aside. But cooler minds prevailed. All the principles Ataturk stood for were eventually collected under a series of increasingly liberal and forward-looking amendments to the first constitution and into succeeding modifications. The last one enacted and the one in effect today is the constitution of 1982.

THE GOVERNMENT

Turkey's government today consists of a single-chamber parliament—the Grand National Assembly—a president who is the head of state, and a Council of Ministers headed by a prime minister. Elections for seats in the Assembly are held every five years, or earlier in some specific cases. The ministers are appointed by the prime minister, who is appointed by the president, who in

Above: Turkey's Grand National Assembly, shown here meeting in Ankara, is the single national legislative body. Left: A Constitutional Court judge hears a case involving Kurdish lawyers. The Constitutional Court is the supreme court of Turkey.

turn is elected by the Assembly. The court system consists of judicial, or criminal, and administrative courts. Cases decided in those courts can be reviewed by the appeals courts and, finally, by the Constitutional Court, over which there is no appeal. This system is totally independent of the other branches of government and political parties. Provincial, municipal, and village authorities, similar to those elsewhere in the West, complete the government.

There are many political parties in Turkey today, but only a handful are important enough to make a difference. Most of these are, at least in name, democratically oriented and claim to adhere fully to the principles espoused by Ataturk.

Turkey remains a friend of the Western democracies Ataturk

befriended. True to the principle of dealing with international issues by peaceful means, Turkey has had to navigate carefully in the muddied waters of its part of the world.

Turkey is near what was, until the early 1990s, the Soviet Union, now Russia and the Commonwealth of Independent States. This nearness was a source of possible conflict because of the common borders, the urge to expand that both former empires had been historically prone to, the deep differences between their philosophies of government, and other problems. Israel and its conflict with the Arab world has been another possible problem for Turkey and its neighbors, because of the Islamic connection.

The revolution in Iran in 1979 brought tension to the area, because Iran turned into a fundamentalist (religion-ruled) state in complete opposition to Turkey with its separation of church and state. Fundamentalists stress following religious rules strictly and literally. The Turkish Welfare Party, which commanded a relative majority in the 1996 elections, leans to religious conservatism and fundamentalism but is equally committed to democratic rule.

Finally, long-standing differences with Greece have continued to smolder for decades. Overall, however, Turkey has managed to maintain respectful and constructive relations with its neighbors.

PLANNING FOR A GROWING ECONOMY

In the 1920s, when the Turkish Republic was established, the country's economy was in total collapse. A bitter war had been fought in its own central territory. The vast outlying territories of the now-extinct Ottoman Empire, which included most of the Balkan Peninsula (Bulgaria, Albania, Greece, and the former

Although Ankara is the capital of Turkey, Istanbul is the financial center. This is the Istanbul headquarters of a major bank.

Yugoslavia), had all been lost as a result of the outcome of World War I. The core of the empire (Istanbul and Anatolia) had traditionally counted on the wealth of its provinces to meet its own needs. For instance, a good part of the empire's industry had been based in its more developed Balkan provinces, while Istanbul had remained essentially an administrative and commercial hub. On the other hand, the agriculture and animal farming that made up practically the entire basis of the Anatolian Peninsula's economy stood at almost prehistoric levels of technical development.

This situation left the new Turkish Republic the task of building up the country's economy. It has been said that the modernization and progress of any one nation has never been more dramatically shown than with Turkey's rise from defeat, chaos, and devastation to the modern nation it is today.

Of course, no one man could have achieved that feat. It was the product of the vision, labors, and dedication of many people—in fact, of the Turkish people as a whole. Ataturk and his followers gave the initial push in the right direction. However, it took much planning and building, erring and correcting, rethinking and restarting, by generations of progressive-thinking Turks, not just to repair Turkey's demolished economy but to build it up into one

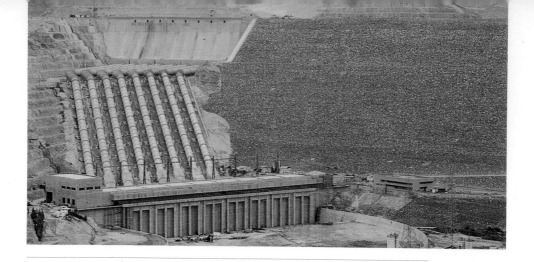

The Ataturk Dam on the Tigris River is now part of Turkey's development of alternative energy sources.

of the strongest in the entire Mediterranean region.

Modern Turkey's economy is still based on agriculture. Almost 45 percent of Turkey's population, which already surpasses the 60 million mark, lives from the land in one way or another. And rightly so, perhaps, since the country is rich in extensive areas of fertile soil, the climate is fairly gentle, and much of the land is still covered with forest growth. Turkey's coastal areas are equally rich in maritime resources. Although it does not have the petroleum deposits found in the Persian Gulf nations to the south, Turkey has valuable industrial raw materials.

At the birth of the republic, there were no roads to carry produce or other loads to the big cities or to the seaports for export. And there was little fuel except for firewood and some coal. There were no alternate energy sources—such as harnessed waterfalls and hydroelectric plants. Unlike most of Europe, Turkey possessed no modern agricultural equipment. But most of all, there was no money. Turkey was bogged down in commitments to repay war debts, and the world's banking system and investors wanted nothing to do with the country.

*Individual women try to improve their own economic situations by selling
embroidery and lace they make to people passing on the road.*

Turkey's new leaders chose not to ask for loans or other types
of financial handouts, even if these had been available. Instead,
they tightened the nation's belt and planned, through thrift and
hard work, to reduce its public and international debt. As a result,
by the mid-twentieth century, Turkey was one of the few countries
in the world that had written off its entire international debt.

From the start, Turkey's leaders used planned economic
development, or "statism," as some called it. The state-run
economies of the Communist countries to the north and east
tended to make grand "five-year plans" for accomplishing its
economic goals. But the Turkish brand of statism differed in one
important respect. Unlike the Communist state-run economies,
which eliminated private enterprise and private property, Turkey's
leaders, instead, promoted private involvement in its national
plans for developing the economy. They fostered the growth of a
Turkish banking system, and they encouraged foreign investment,
although they were not always consistent in that.

Turkey's first planning stages started soon after the creation of the republic, but they were limited, experimental affairs, mostly geared to developing industry. Then, during World War II, there was a period devoid of any planning whatsoever. After their bad experience with choosing sides in World War I, the Turks hesitated almost throughout the war between plunging into the fray and remaining neutral. They chose neutrality until the very end, when Turkey joined the Allies. Economic planning was resumed after the war, and, in 1961, a new constitution made planning a mandatory constitutional requirement.

The first three "five-year development plans," stretching from 1963 to 1977, proved extremely successful. During the first, an average annual rate of growth of the economy was 6.7 percent, compared to the stated goal of 7 percent. But during the second and third periods, the average rates of growth were 7.2 percent and 8.5 percent. The 8.5 percent was attained despite the economic shock that set in when spiraling oil prices hit the economies of all fuel-consuming countries in the world.

Three more five-year plans were interspersed with two one-year, interim plans. In each, the public and private sectors of the economy were treated as complementary to each other. This view resulted in broad private ownership of business. It also intensified the exploitation of land and national resources by including hitherto landless peasants and workers in all development plans. Additional goals of the five-year plans included promotion of technical training and scientific education, advancement toward a healthy balance of external payments, and the encouragement of industrial growth in order to reduce the country's dependence on imports.

Agriculture is the mainstay of the Turkish economy. Many hillsides have been terraced in order to increase the amount of good farmland. These workers are picking tea.

In the 1970s, however, the oil crisis, foreign-exchange difficulties, and other worldwide problems adversely affected the Turkish economy. As a result, in early 1980, a new set of economic goals was enacted. These "January 24 Decisions" went even further in the direction of freeing the economy from excessive government regulation. Coupled to the new 1982 constitution, these measures contributed greatly to increased development and to the political and social stability of the country. Even so, by the mid-1990s, other factors, including the war in Bosnia, terrorism, and worldwide economic uncertainties, were again troubling the Turkish economy.

AGRICULTURE AND OTHER RESOURCES

Turkey is a world leader in the production of cereals, wheat, barley, and maize (corn), and in leguminous crops such as lentils, chickpeas, and beans. Some of Turkey's crops—sugar beets, tea leaves, coffee beans, cotton, and tobacco—are highly renowned for

Although Turkey has considerable deposits of coal, much of it is so deep that it is costly to extract. These workers (left) are in a coal mine in Elazig. Sunflowers (right) are among the oil-producing plants grown in Turkey.

quality as well as their quantity. The country is a world leader in cotton production, as well as that of olive, sunflower-seed, and peanut oils. Turkey is also a world leader in producing grapes and figs, and its crops of citrus fruits, apples, and hazelnuts are important. Its garden produce is both varied and plentiful. Turkey stands sixth in the world in number of sheep (over fifty million head) and is a leader in milk and wool production, poultry and eggs, and other products from livestock.

Along Turkey's long coastline and its plentiful lakes and rivers, the fishing industry produces anchovies, mackerel, sardines, and bluefish, as well as other abundant products. In addition, the many reservoirs or artificial lakes created by its vast program of dam construction have contributed to both the agricultural potential of underdeveloped areas and the development of an even larger fisheries industry.

Almost 40 percent of the country's territory is covered with rich and productive forests. These areas are being increasingly tapped for export purposes as well as for use in local construction, furniture, and paper industries. Road and railroad construction has forged ahead in recent years, and alternative energy sources are being developed.

MINING AND INDUSTRY

Turkey's industrial output has increased dramatically in recent years. Though nowhere near as rich in fossil fuels as its oil-rich neighbors to the south, Turkey has still managed to substantially develop its petrochemical industry. In 1972 Turkey exported only 5 percent as much as it imported in chemicals and petrochemicals combined. By 1989 the ratio of exports to imports in this sector had improved to about 70 percent. Exports of manufactured consumer goods already outweigh imports. These goods include processed foods, fabric, clothing, beverages, leather goods, furniture, shoes, and tobacco. In the area of materials used in manufacturing—iron and steel, processed forest products, glass, plastics, cement, and petrochemicals—the industry is fast catching up with the demand. However, in road vehicles, metalware, electronics, heavy machinery, and agricultural equipment, there is a lag, but industry is making headway to meet future needs.

Turkey has significant mineral resources, including granite and marble, magnesite, boron salts, barite, chromium, copper, iron, thorium (reportedly 70 percent of the worldwide reserves), hard coal, lignite, asphaltite, tungsten, crude oil, nickel, and manganese. These riches are being exploited more fully as new, more modern

Turkey provides tourists with
many diverse opportunities
both for sightseeing and for
relaxation (counterclockwise
from above): Hadrian's Temple
at Ephesus near Kusadasi; the
thermal springs at Pamukkale;
swimming off sandy beaches;
and modern hotels.

methods of extraction are used and numerous hydroelectric plants are built to power the operations.

SERVICES

As in many countries around the world, Turkey's most dramatic economic growth has taken place in service industries. These include such economic activities as transportation, banking/insurance/finance, construction, hotels and restaurants, tourism, culture and entertainment, as well as education and administration. The increased efficiency of Turkish industry and agriculture has meant a decrease in the manpower needed to maintain those areas, freeing workers to take advantage of the newer arena of the service industries.

Tourism, in particular, has had a truly amazing development in recent decades, though it was affected by wars in the region. Turkey is fortunate in having wonderful places to visit, and its treasure of architectural monuments and archeological remains is endless. But Turkey also has developed its hotel and restaurant facilities, both at traditionally tourist areas such as beaches and in more remote areas of the interior.

Tourism authorities now promote not only historical and architectural tourism, but such specialty types of travel as mountaineering and nature tourism, health tourism (thermal, or hot water, spas), whitewater rafting, and fishing and hunting. In 1992, the number of visitors to Turkey was just slightly under six million, bringing in revenues of $2.9 billion. Such growth— 40 percent over the previous year—will probably happen again and again as travelers discover Turkey's many and varied assets.

Above: These women in Ankara wear Western-style clothes and enjoy ice cream.
Below: In the village of Urgup, a woman carries her child while leading a donkey.

Chapter 5

EVERYDAY LIFE

There is no way to describe the everyday life of a typical Turk because actually there is no typical Turk. Perhaps the most generalized characteristic of the Turkish population is their religion—Islam—yet some are fundamentalist and some are Muslims in name only. Over 98 percent of the population are Muslims, mostly of the Sunni branch, though many others follow the Shiite branch.

There are greater differences between a Muslim farmer in the hinterlands of Anatolia and a Muslim office worker in Ankara than between a Muslim shopkeeper in Istanbul's Grand Bazaar and his Jewish counterpart in the shops of the Beyoglu district.

Though the Jewish and Christian religious minorities are small, they are important economically and culturally. Totally free to worship according to the tenets of their faiths, they enjoy the same political rights guaranteed to all Turkish people. Mostly they concentrate in such large cities as Istanbul, Ankara, and Izmir.

When Turkey took on a nonreligious government, it adopted the Western solar calendar for all nonreligious purposes. Therefore, the school weekend is Saturday and Sunday, Sunday and sometimes part of Saturday being the day of rest for store, factory, and office workers. School vacations are in summer, with a shorter midyear break in the early spring.

*Left: Women in a traditional Islamic school learn Arabic and study the Qur'an.
Right: At Middle East Technical University in Ankara, scientific subjects are
studied in English.*

WHAT IS A TURK?

Aside from religion, the other unifying element is the Turkish
language. It is spoken by practically all Turkish citizens and is the
mother tongue to at least 90 percent of the people. Modern Turkish
is derived in part from the old Turkic languages spoken by the
ancestral tribes originating in Central Asia. The language was later
consolidated as Ottoman Turkish and enriched with many Persian
and Arabic words and phrases. Since the proclamation of the
republic, however, many foreign influences have been dropped
from the language. Turkey abandoned the use of Arabic script and
adopted Latin script for its written form.

The main minority linguistic groups in Turkey are the Kurds
and Arabs. Kurdish is the mother tongue of some 6 percent of the
population, concentrated mostly in rural areas of eastern and
southeastern Anatolia. There are many Kurds living in the large
western population centers as well, but they have largely been
absorbed into the mainstream of the country's people.

Turkish guards protect supplies at a Kurdish refugee station at Uludare.

The so-called Kurdish problem has been a worrisome matter in recent Turkish history. It is a very complex issue. Many Kurds would like to form their own separate state. Large numbers of Kurds have fled into Turkey from surrounding territories—Iran, Iraq, and Russia's southernmost areas. Guerrilla fighting by the Kurds has been going on since the 1980s and has drained energy from Turkey's plans for development. The solution to this problem is yet to be found.

The Arabic population in Turkey is much smaller than the Kurdish. It is concentrated in parts of southeastern Anatolia adjacent to Syria and Iraq. Greek and Armenian are spoken by small but significant pockets of people concentrated principally in the larger cities, mainly Istanbul. The Jewish population has mostly adopted Turkish for everyday purposes, but they maintain by tradition the use of their languages of origin. For example, Sephardic Spanish is spoken by those descended from the Jews

expelled by Spain in the fifteenth century, and Yiddish by those descended from northern European emigrants.

Given the region's history, it is also difficult to define a typical ethnic Turk. Turkey has been in the very center of the movements of people across continents, invasions, and trading routes for so many centuries that its present-day inhabitants abound in traits from the peoples of all of Eurasia. They may exhibit characteristics of the Gauls and Italians from the west, Greeks and Macedonians from the north, Persians and Arabs from the south, and Mongol peoples from the east. These last left the strongest traces on the population, at least regarding language. But the result has been a diverse group, conveniently categorized as Mediterranean-Turkic. Within the group, it is as easy to find a blue-eyed blonde or red-haired Turk as it is to spot a stocky round-headed Alpine individual or a long-headed Italo-Mediterranean one or the high-cheekboned dark Mongol type.

As populations have moved and shifted across Turkey, they have occupied farms, towns, and great cities. Opposite page, far left: a family home in Koycegiz; left: a Kurdish farmhouse in Kurdistan. Right: crowded apartment houses in Istanbul.

POPULATION GROWTH

Although Turkey is not heavily populated by European standards, the population has grown rapidly in recent decades. The nation has sustained a high birth rate, which has combined with a decreasing death rate as a result of improved health and medical standards. By the mid-1990s, the country's total population approached sixty-five million, compared with less than fourteen million in 1927.

A large portion of this population is concentrated in major cities. Istanbul has a population exceeding ten million. Ankara, the capital, has close to four million and Izmir, over three million. At least three other cities—Bursa, Konya, and Adana—have passed the million mark.

The rapid growth of the country's cities is the consequence of the government's plans aimed at promoting industrial activity, as well as the natural growth of the services sector of the economy.

The 40 percent of the population that is still rural is the most traditional and conservative, while the city-living people have become increasingly Westernized in their ways.

Contributing to the movement of people to cities has been the government's intensive development of mass housing, especially in the cities. As rural people have lost jobs to the mechanization of agriculture, they have had to move to cities to find jobs. And the new jobs are increasingly available in the service industries developing in the urban areas.

WOMEN AND THE TURKISH FAMILY

After the proclamation of the republic, one of the pillars of the new order was the principle of egalitarianism. Equal rights and privileges were guaranteed to all Turkish citizens, regardless of sex, religion, or ethnic origins. Perhaps in the case of women's rights, the changes brought about by Ataturk have been most revolutionary and far-reaching. At the end of the nineteenth century, women's rights were already being modernized by the

An upper-class Turkish woman of a hundred years ago might have smoked a water pipe.

Although the republic has been secular for many decades, many Islamic women still wear traditional head coverings, while others wear Western clothing. The women above were photographed in the 1970s; the woman and her children at right in the 1990s.

more enlightened Ottoman sultans. Slavery and the practice of owning concubines were prohibited as far back as 1847. But until the twentieth century, polygamy (the right of a man to have more than one legal wife) was common. Woman's place in the family, and in the realm of things in general, was decided by religious practice and belief.

In the 1920s, it was decided to secularize the state—to declare it independent from the mandates of any one religion. That fact, plus the constitutional principle of equality under the law for all Turks, had the effect of instantly placing Turkish women on a par with Turkish men in every sense.

In the cities, the new laws immediately meant the abandonment of the restrictive dress code for women, equal opportunities for education, and equal pay for identical jobs in the public sector. Small villages and rural areas were another matter. The "traditional" living style and social relations remained as they

Girls often have different opportunities depending on the degree of Westernization of their families. Those on the left are city girls on playground equipment. Those above study in an Islamic school in eastern Turkey.

were for many decades: all individuals economically dependent on the family and under the almost absolute rule of the father. The old dress code for women was still followed, even if the all-concealing veil itself was usually dropped. And this is still the case in some rural areas of modern Turkey.

A more Westernized type of family life has become common in the cities. Families are generally smaller now, as the younger generations freely choose to leave their father's shelter to start families of their own. Earning a living has become more important in social relations than submission to the old-style family patterns.

Women themselves have done a lot to further their equality. Through organizations for the defense of women's status and their own increased activity as journalists, business leaders, educators, and political leaders, women have brought about fruitful progress. Polygamy is now a thing of the past. Inheritance rights for both women and men have been made equal. Political activity is open to both men and women. In fact, in the mid-1990s, Turkey's prime minister was a woman, Tansu Ciller. She later took on the job of minister of foreign affairs in a coalition government with the Muslim traditionalist-oriented Welfare Party. Job opportunities are equally (at least in theory, as in other Western societies) open to both.

YOUTH AND SPORTS

Because of its high birth rate, Turkey is a country of young people, and the issues of the younger generations have become a primary concern of the government. In 1986 the country's general directorate of youth and sports was reorganized and given increased responsibilities.

Among the directorate's responsibilities are the promotion of scouting activities and the establishment of youth camps. The aim is to provide leisure facilities for young people, to train them in good

The Turkish government has recognized the importance of traditional folk dancing and gives it financial support and encouragement.

citizenship, and to introduce them to the country's natural resources. The directorate also helps to preserve and recover traditional folk dancing and folk music. By the mid-1990s, almost half a million young people in the country participated in these activities. The government organizes youth festivals and chess tournaments and establishes youth centers in villages and sports facilities in all significant population centers.

Football (the European type, known in the United States as soccer) is Turkey's most popular sport, both for spectators and players. Some of Turkey's professional football teams, including Istanbul's oldest club, the Galatasaray, have excelled in international competition. Turks are generally sports-minded, making them active in such sports as athletics, archery, basketball, wrestling and grease wrestling, weight lifting and body building, fencing, handball, karate and judo, table tennis, shooting, tennis, and volleyball. The country is rich in mountainous areas and coastline, so many people enjoy mountaineering, whitewater rafting, skiing, yachting, swimming, and underwater sports.

EDUCATION

All children are required to go through the primary and intermediate levels, grades one through eight. Schools are largely public and free, though private schooling also is offered. Nursery school and kindergarten are available for little children. And secondary and higher learning centers, such as professional or technical schools and universities, are widespread.

The secondary education level is offered at various types of *lycées,* or "high schools," and other technical schools where

Istanbul University is one of nearly fifty universities in Turkey. University students have a history of trying to bring about social change.

students can be trained in anything—secretarial skills to basic sciences, teaching to tourism, hotel skills to trade or technical skills. Secondary students can also prepare for higher education.

There are nearly fifty universities in Turkey, some of them private, in addition to many other higher professional learning centers and institutes. They are all attached to and coordinated through the Higher Education Council. Their total number of students stood close to one million by the mid-1990s. Foreign students, numbering close to twenty thousand at that time, can enter Turkish universities upon approval of an examination. It is similar to the test required for Turkish applicants, but it is handed out to the foreigner in both English and Turkish. If the applicant is approved but has little knowledge of Turkish, he or she is given a year in which to gain proficiency in the language before starting actual courses.

Turkish universities are required and paid by the state to carry out scientific research. Research is being carried out in such fields as health, solar energy, marine sciences, ecology, biomedicine, engineering, accident prevention, fine arts, and television and cinema. These programs are supported both publicly and privately.

FOODS OF TURKEY

Turkey's culinary art is particularly rich because of all the territories and traditions the Ottomans could draw from at the heyday of the empire. It also benefits from fresh produce hauled into the towns and cities daily from the rich farmlands.

Some of the more famous Turkish specialties are the rice or *pilaf* dishes, mostly served with meat or seafood, such as chunks of lamb, mussels, or shrimp. All kinds of vegetable dishes, but particularly the delicious eggplant specialties, are also popular. One famous dish, *imambayildi,* consists simply of eggplant and olive oil. Its name means "the imam fainted"—perhaps from marveling at the tastiness of the dish. (An *imam* is an Islamic religious leader.) *Dolma* is vine or cabbage leaves filled with meat and wrapped up into delicious little bundles.

Turkey is most famous for its desserts. Its European-style pastries leave nothing to be desired even when compared with

As in many countries, both cooked and natural foods are available in the open markets: at left, a woman of Izmir selling olives; at right, a man tending the cooking of lamb on a turning spit.

Vienna's best. Perhaps the most famous pastry is *baklavah*, many thin layers of flaky pastry between layers of walnuts and olive oil. Turkish rice pudding, or *sutlac*, is popular, as is *samsa*, a flaky pastry with walnuts, hazelnuts, or almonds. Two exotic dishes are *kadin gobegi*, "lady's navel," and *dilber dudagi*, "beauty's lips." But the most famous Turkish treat of all is *lokum*, or "Turkish delight," made of such simple ingredients as honey and flour, or just plain sugar and wheat starch.

Turkey's wines are quite good and varied, the aniseed-flavored *raki* being the most famous. Excellent tea, served in table-sized samovars, is a universal day-long drink at all levels of society. And, of course, Turkey's rich, thick, and blackest coffee is world famous.

The holiest spot in all Islam is the Ka'bah, or Kaaba, a temple in Mecca,
where Muhammad was born. Millions of pilgrims come to Mecca every year.

Chapter 6

ISLAM—THE
RELIGIOUS LIFE

Religion is a matter of enormous importance to the Turkish people, even if separation of church and state is perhaps the most evident single fact of modern Turkey, unlike other Muslim countries. Over 98 percent of the Turkish people are Muslims, and the religion they follow is called Islam. Islam developed from the teachings of Muhammad, a holy man born in the Arabian Peninsula, who lived in the sixth and seventh centuries A.D.

Islam is the last of the world's great religions to arise. Like both Judaism and Christianity, from which it arose, Islam has the belief that there is only one God. Many prophets and holy figures of Judaism and Christianity are also considered prophets of Allah, the one god of Islam. Jesus is considered the next to the last prophet and Muhammad is the last.

Before the surge of Islam, the peoples of Arabia followed many different religious practices based on animism (belief in gods identified with either animals or objects) or tribal myths. They saw gods in specific animals or in the family heroes of their ancestors related to them through oral tradition. Some felt the influence of Judeo-Christian traditions and preaching that came out of Jerusalem and other cities to the north. But most Arabs were people living

Muhammad, the founding prophet of Islam, is shown in this old engraving. However, the traditions of Islam make it wrong for an artist to make an illustration of a human figure.

either in small villages or wandering as nomads tending their flocks. Their various faiths had not yet jelled into a formal body of religious thought.

THE LAST PROPHET

Before the seventh century A.D., in the valley of Mecca in present-day Saudi Arabia, a relatively prosperous community worshiped the site of divinity in a small temple, called the Ka'bah. The Ka'bah was a sort of boxlike temple which all the gods, including Jewish and Christian figures and icons, were supposed to inhabit. This territory had become sacred and free from invasions or plundering by the surrounding tribes.

It was into one of the lesser clans inhabiting Mecca that Muhammad was born in the year 570. An orphan raised by relatives, he spent his formative years living a nomadic life in the desert. There he learned to reflect and contemplate. Still, as a young man he excelled in the normal pursuits of youth and became a reasonably successful trader. Apparently he also had a knack for impressing women. One of them, Khadijah, his rich employer from one of the main clans of the tribe, was smitten by him and offered him marriage.

As he moved into his forties, Muhammad reflected on matters of good and evil, plenty and poverty, justice and greed, and the lack of direction and organization he saw around him. He had a vision of a majestic being coming to him and addressing him as "the messenger of God." Muhammad later identified this presence as that of the Archangel Gabriel and, for many years thereafter, he continued receiving revelations that he declared came from Allah —God—through Gabriel. Told to share these revelations with his people, Muhammad set about doing so. In less than a dozen years, he succeeded in swinging many people to a belief in a single deity, whose essence was a combination of power, goodness, and generosity. However, some of the more powerful people in Mecca decided Muhammad was dangerous.

Rather than fight, in 622 Muhammad and his followers emigrated to Medina, a town about 300 miles (483 kilometers) north of Mecca. Muhammad set up his capital there. This exodus, called the *hegira,* marks the start of the Muslim calendar. Even so, Muhammad did not disown Mecca, but reaffirmed its sacred essence as the central point for the worship of Allah. Through the following years, the Ka'bah in Mecca was cleared of effigies and symbols of older and minor deities and became dedicated solely to Allah, while the group of people that originally opposed Muhammad's innovative teachings were rapidly drawn to his cause, attracted by the reports that spread from Medina of his success there.

THE SEED OF DIVISION

Muhammad died at the height of his success, in 632, without having openly appointed a successor, called a caliph, to take over his leadership. From his marriage with Khadijah, Muhammad had had two surviving daughters. One daughter, Fatimah, had married Ali, a cousin of Muhammad. Many felt the prophet had already designated Ali privately as his chosen successor. Others, however, particularly those in Mecca, believed Ali would not be a good choice. Instead, they elected another trusted and worthy follower who would be more amenable to members of the community. This was Abu Bakr, Muhammad's father-in-law by one of his younger wives.

Though this last choice prevailed momentarily, the seed of division had been planted. It was to become the source of later conflict that continues to this day, between two of the main branches of Islam. The Muslims called *Sunnis* follow "the clear and well-trodden path" of the majority, who chose Abu Bakr. The *Shiites* still claim that it was Ali's rights and those of his sons (Muhammad's grandsons) that should have prevailed.

In Turkey, most Muslims are Sunni. Those of Turkey's neighbor to the south, Iran, are mainly Shiite. This difference accounts for considerable tension between the two countries.

THE SPREAD OF ISLAM

Muhammad's revelations were collected after his death into the book known as the Qur'an, or Koran. His teachings reaffirmed much of the contents of the Judeo-Christian Bible and testaments.

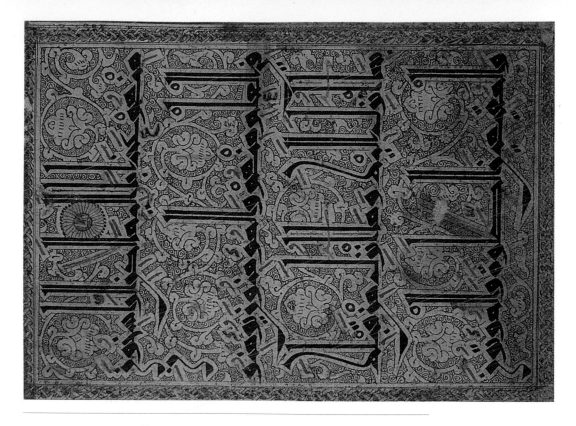

This page from an illuminated (illustrated) Qur'an dates from the eleventh century, approximately the date by which the Turkish people had converted to Islam.

Muhammad recognized a special status for the followers of the faiths of Moses and Jesus, into which he also gathered his own followers. Islam spread from Arabia with amazing speed. Sometimes it did so by "moral persuasion," and often through warfare and invasions.

By the eleventh century, Islam had already been adopted in Turkey. When the Ottoman Turks finally arose, they gave new energy and vitality to the Islamic faith. The Ottomans became the greatest builders in Muslim history. Without doubt, Turkey boasts the largest number of, and largest, mosques in the whole of Islam, though other countries—especially Spain, Egypt, and Iran—have mosques of great beauty and charm. Through the Ottomans' expansion of their empire, they spread Islam to include all of Asia Minor, many territories to the east, and even large parts of Europe.

THE FAITH OF ISLAM

It is difficult to summarize the complex faith of Islam. But the main points of the faith are easily recognizable to people of other faiths. Some are:

God is unique and omnipotent.

He is just and merciful.

God is close to humankind as a personal God.

God is the creator of the universe and designer of the order of all things.

With their capacity to obey and disobey (free will), humans hold a superior status in this order.

Satan is a fallen angel and dedicated to leading humans astray.

Humans are subject to the cardinal sin of pride, which fills us with disobedience and the assumption that we may be either Godless or in partnership with God, rather than God's instrument.

The words and deeds or miracles of the prophets are to be believed. They were such as Abraham, Noah, Moses, Jesus, and Muhammad himself, all of whom are considered men and not divine, and who do not receive the revelations directly from God but through angels or messengers.

The Suleymaniye Mosque in Istanbul is one of the mosques designed by sixteenth-century architect Mimar Sinan. One of its main towers, or minarets, shown enlarged on the opposite page, is where the muezzin, *or crier, announces when it is time for all good Muslims to pray.*

Social service and social responsibility or generosity, or brotherhood, or community of faith make up an important principle.

The *jihad*, or the struggle involving the use of armed force, is acceptable whenever necessary to protect the faith.

Finally, there will be a last day, or day of judgment, when the dead shall be resurrected, the just rewarded with the pleasures of Paradise, and the unrepentant sinners condemned to the fires of Hell, both physically and "in their hearts."

Muhammad's ideal had an amazing humane effect on the violent society of his time. Slavery, though not outlawed, was regulated, and slaves were given legal rights, including the right to purchase their freedom from their earnings. Infanticide, or the killing of unwanted newborn girls, was forbidden. The poor were guaranteed to be helped by the required daily good deeds of those with means. Distinctions and privileges based on tribal rank or race were repudiated, and all men were declared to be the "equal children of Adam," the only distinction in the sight of God to be based on piety and good acts. Until Muhammad's time, a person guilty of murder could pay a surrogate, or substitute, to be executed in his place. This terrible practice was abolished.

In general, the pre-Islamic ideal of manliness as having to do with ruthless, violent boldness gave way to a greatly modified and more humane ideal based on virtue, piety, and good deeds.

THE FIVE PILLARS

The articles of faith imply adherence to certain basic actions which are perhaps the better-known signs of Islam to the Western observer. Called the "Five Pillars of Islam," they are:

1. The profession of faith: "There is no god but Allah and Muhammad is His Prophet." This profession must be recited at least once in a Muslim's lifetime, aloud, correctly, and purposefully, with full understanding of its meaning, and the assent from the heart.

2. Prayer. To be said five times a day, from before sunrise to bedtime, if possible in a gathering or at the mosque. It also involves the washing of hands, face, and feet each time. In practice, prayers are conducted on Fridays at the larger mosques. At the side of every mosque in Turkey there runs a long basin with dozens, if not hundreds, of water spouts or faucets that the faithful

Prayer to Allah is one of the Five Pillars of Islam. Even out on a distant country road, the faithful gather to face Mecca and pray five times a day (above). Prayer beads (right) may be used to help the recitation of the ritual prayers.

use just before the *muezzin*, or crier, calls them to prayer from the mosque's *minaret*, or tower. Today many mosques have substituted the muezzin's appearance at the top of the minaret with a blaring electric public-address system. The faithful, arranged behind the *imam*, all face Mecca, then pray a set of recitations aloud. The prayer is marked by bows and prostrations, with the faithful bringing their brows down to the ground.

3. Purification or *zakat*. The third pillar stands for the tax or contribution due to Islam. It is levied on the faithful's possessions at certain pre-established percentages, running from about 2 to 10 percent, depending on the goods assessed (cash, jewels, grain, cattle, etc.). The proceeds are for the poor, or for people ridden

Left: Faithful Muslims learn to read Arabic in order to read the holy book, or Qur'an (or Koran), in its original language.
Above: Faithful Muslims also hope to be able to go to Mecca at least once in the lifetime to pray at the Ka'bah, the holy Black Stone believed to be the only remains of an altar built by Abraham.

with chronic debt, or (in olden times and as mentioned in the Qur'an) for the ransom of war captives. This tax is intended to purify one's remaining wealth.

4. Fasting. Fasting takes place during the month of Ramadan, the ninth month of the Muslims' lunar year. The month starts with the sighting by reliable witnesses the night before of the crescent moon. Then, no eating, drinking, smoking, or sexual intercourse can take place from before sunrise to after sundown. A secondary

duty of the faithful during Ramadan is the daily feeding of a poor person.

5. The *Hajj*, or annual pilgrimage to Mecca. The time for the pilgrimage falls at the beginning of the last month of the Muslim year and it must be undertaken by every Muslim, "provided one can afford it" and families are provided for, once in a lifetime. In practice, however, not all good Muslims make the trip, since currency and border restrictions may make the trip to Saudi Arabia impossible. Still, with the prevalence of air travel and other facilities, well over a million Muslims foreign to Saudi Arabia, including many from Turkey, visit the Ka'bah at Mecca each year.

Aside from the Five Pillars, Islamic thought and practice emphasize family life. To this end, the institution of marriage is central, and chastity in women (and in men to a lesser extent) out of wedlock is of paramount importance. Filial respect to the father figure and tenderness to the mother are equally important. The life of every Muslim is to be dedicated to the performance of religious rites and duties and active good deeds.

In today's Turkey, of course, given the modernizing trend and secularism adopted at the formation of the republic, many of these articles of faith and practice have become diluted in large sectors of the Muslim population. In others they have been accentuated. In recent years, fundamentalist Muslims have won both municipal and national elections. However, electoral results, even if apparently related to religious causes, may have had just as much to do with questions of political ethics and the general economic picture. After the 1996 elections, the fundamentalists agreed to moderate their religious stance so as to be able to govern through a coalition with one of the larger secular political parties.

While a cat listens and watches, an old man plays his flute for passersby at the Blue Mosque in Istanbul.

Chapter 7

THE CULTURAL SCENE

Turkey's cultural scene is very much like one of its famed centuries-old carpets—unequaled in the richness and intricacy of its design. Or it's like the fragrant and delicious blend of cooking traditions picked up from the many regions in the vast Ottoman Empire of its past. But, if anything, it is the mixture of old and new that is the most striking.

ARCHITECTURE

The Ottomans excelled particularly in the art and techniques of construction. Their forebears, the Seljuk Turks, had already greatly developed the art and created important buildings such as caravanseries, theological schools, mosques, and mausoleums, of which there are many samples left in Anatolia. But with the conquest of Constantinople, the Ottomans discovered the dome-building skills of the Byzantines, and they adopted this technique for building their mosques and palaces.

A unique sample of palace architecture is the famed Topkapi Palace in Istanbul. Started by Sultan Mehmet II after his conquest of the great Roman city in 1453, it became a vast complex of domed buildings and courtyards. Many of its additions were not completed until nearly three centuries later. Today it is a museum

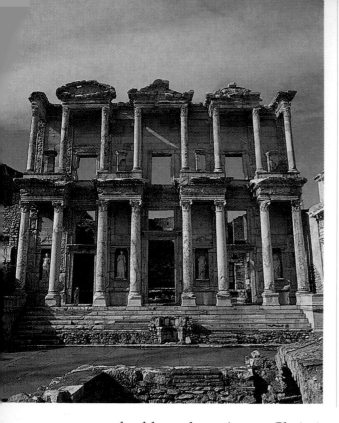

Architectural examples abound in Turkey from throughout history. These ruins of the Library of Celsus are located at the ancient city of Ephesus.

housing priceless art, jewels, and furniture from the past.

One of the greatest Ottoman architects was Mimar Sinan, who adapted the Byzantine tradition as his own. He actually had been born into a Christian family and was recruited into the Janissaries' corporation. He left more than three hundred beautiful buildings in Istanbul, Edirne, and places as far away as Hungary to the northwest and Tunisia to the southwest. Possibly his greatest creation was the Suleymaniye Mosque in Istanbul, a great mosque with four minarets and a wealth of mosaic work. It encompasses theological schools and the tombs of Suleyman and Roxelane, a beautiful Russian concubine whom Suleyman had married against custom and tradition. There also is a more modest tomb for Sinan himself.

Sinan's perfection of design and his mastery in the combination of space and masses influenced architectural styles for centuries. But in the latter part of the eighteenth and in the nineteenth centuries, architects looked toward the West, and largely baroque, overly decorated or garish, elements became prevalent. One of Europe's most glaringly ornate palaces, the Dolmabahce Palace on

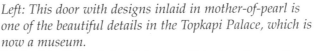

Left: This door with designs inlaid in mother-of-pearl is one of the beautiful details in the Topkapi Palace, which is now a museum.
Right: The Dolmabahce Palace, built in the nineteenth century during the decline of the Ottoman Empire, uses the extra-fancy ornament of the Western baroque style.

the shores of the Bosporus, was built to the glory of the waning Ottomans. It boasts such things as the heaviest crystal chandelier in the world (weighing over 4 tons), a throne room with a 115-foot (35-meter)-wide dome above it, and furnishings to make other palaces pale by comparison.

The republic, however, has brought about an upsurge of contemporary styles based on function and practicality rather than the sumptuousness favored of old. Still, successive governments have continued to regard as important the restoration and maintenance of buildings and monuments from the past.

The "whirling dervishes" were Muslim monks who thought they moved closer to Allah by dancing themselves into trances. Their performances contributed to the traditional Turkish theater.

LITERATURE AND PERFORMING ARTS

Before turning to Islam, Turkic literature was mostly oral. The sagas of tribal history and heroes were transmitted by word of mouth from generation to generation in vigorous and poetic style. Some inscriptions have been preserved from the seventh and eighth centuries, engraved onto obelisks and other monumental works. They show the beauty of the oral poets' language.

With Islam came the easy and delicate mastery of language developed by the Arabs and Persians. For centuries, most writing used the classical and elegant styles found in Islamic poetry, while the folk styles continued to be used for epic stories. In recent

Three men play traditional Turkish instruments on the railway platform in the city of Edirne, near the Greek border.

times, literature and drama have been influenced by the West, and many creative talents have arisen in all areas of literature, from the novel and short story to the social essay, mystical poetry, lyric poetry, and the drama.

Theater has flourished in the modern republic. This may be partly because drama had long been a literary tradition in old Turkey. The people improvised epic plays, gave shadow-theater performances, and absorbed the ceremonies of the religious people known as "whirling dervishes." The dervishes are a mystical order of Islamic monks of the Sufi order, dating back to the thirteenth century. They believed in expressing their philosophy, based on purity of heart, peace with one's self and the universe at large, and

Turks have an ancient heritage of theater, stemming from the productions put on in large Greek amphitheaters. Turkey has the ruins of several such amphitheaters.

man's search for perfection, by ritual dancing.

Opera performances are especially popular. Istanbul's State Opera offers a wide range of operatic productions, as well as ballet performances. During Istanbul's International Festival, held every year in June and July, Mozart's *The Abduction from the Seraglio* is staged right at the Topkapi Palace, precisely where the action of the opera is supposed to take place. There are many theaters in Istanbul, Ankara, and other cities dedicated to staging the plays of world literature aside from those by Turkish authors.

Music in Turkey is also a blend of many cultures and styles. Both Persian and Byzantine influences predominate in the traditional folk music and dances. There are many schools and performing groups around the country devoted to continuing Turkey's musical traditions. However, there are equally as many conservatories, major orchestral groups, and institutions dedicated to traditional classical Western music. And as for popular music, in the urban areas particularly, anything goes, from the Charleston or the tango to the rumba or just plain American or Turkish pop.

The modern Turkish cinema is an art form that has developed rapidly in recent decades. Turkey is today one of the most prolific movie-making nations, and in the 1970s produced over three hundred films a year, though few were of great quality. More recently, movie production has decreased, but the quality has improved considerably. Turkey's most renowned filmmaker of the past was Muksin Ertugul, whose influence is still felt today.

There are many schools and institutions that specialize in training for careers in the cinema industry, including Istanbul's Mimar Sinan University, the University of Ankara, and others. Production for television, which has a dozen channels, has become increasingly important.

PLASTIC ARTS AND MUSEUMS

Painting was never one of the great Turkish traditions, mostly because of Islam's opposition to the picturing of likenesses of living beings. However, in recent times, much interest has sprung up among the Turks, especially after many young Turks were sent to Paris by the

The Greek heritage is also found in the smaller details, such as this panel of bas-relief sculpture.

A mosaic of Jesus and his Apostles highlights the domed ceiling of Kariye Byzantine Church, which is now a museum.

Ottoman sultans and prosperous families to gain sophistication and worldliness. Turkish painting has thus gone through approximately the same phases that Western art has gone through, with impressionism, expressionism, cubism, surrealism, nonrepresentational art, primitivism, and back to neoclassical realism, succeeding, or intermingling with, each other during the past century. And the same is the case with sculpture.

There are many art galleries in the cities of Istanbul, Ankara, and Izmir. There are, as well, excellent museums where the artistic wealth of centuries has been collected. The first museums in Turkey date back to the mid-nineteenth century. Today there are nearly five hundred museum buildings and open-air museums in Turkey. They display millions of works of art and the architectural and archeological remains of the civilizations that

Little has changed in centuries in the way a Turkish silk rug is woven. Such rugs are highly valued the world over.

flourished in this land, from pre-Byzantine times to today's modern Turks.

Some of the main museums are the Archaeological Museums in both Istanbul and Ankara, the Turkish and Islamic Art Museum and the Painting and Sculpture Museum in Istanbul, the Anatolian Civilizations Museum in Ankara. Also in Ankara is the Ataturk Mausoleum, dedicated to the memory of Mustafa Kemal Ataturk.

CARPET WEAVING AND MORE

The weaving of rugs or carpets for floors as well as wall coverings is one of the great traditional arts of the Turkish people. Their excellence in this area came to them from the Seljuks and, even earlier, their Turkic-Mongol ancestors. However, the Persian influence introduced refinements that continue to distinguish the Turkish product. Although the carpets from Persia are perhaps best known for their delicacy and intricacy of design, those of Turkey boast a matchless majesty of subject and rare depth of color. As with most good Islamic art, the depiction of living beings is seldom attempted, except in rugs woven commercially for the Western taste.

At a "carpet farm," newly made carpets are laid out in the sun to make the colors fade and become more "mellow."

Turkish rugs are made of cotton, wool, or silk. The most intricate in design and hardest to produce are silk, requiring the tying of hundreds of knots per 1 square inch (6.4 square centimeters). These are mostly small prayer rugs or wall hangings, and they are often the most expensive ones produced today.

The finest and most highly priced rugs are woolen ones from the fifteenth through the seventeenth centuries originating in the Anatolian highlands. They use bold colors to show stars, polygons, and other geometric figures, and sometimes ornate patterns intended to suggest birds or animals, though not to depict them realistically. The great Flemish and German painters of the Renaissance, such as Hans Memling, Jan van Eyck, and Hans Holbein, depicted these carpets in their detailed indoor oil portraits. Today the traditional Anatolian designs are still used with little change by girls weaving in their ancestral villages across the land. Some of the best known of Turkey's rugs come from the towns and regions of Ghiordes and Kula (both particularly well

This woman in Cappadocia displays one of the many artistic crafts that are part of the lives of Turkish people.

known for their prayer rugs), Usak, Goreme, Ladik, Milas, Konya, Kirsehir, and Kars.

The decorative arts have always been popular. They are part of the Ottoman tradition of luxury, and they conform as well to the Turkish people's dexterity in the arts and crafts in general.

The making of miniatures—painting or embroidering on a very small scale—comes from the old Seljuk traditions but was reinforced by the Persians. In this art, the human figure blends in with landscape and realistic backgrounds in a manner curiously winked at by Islamic fundamentalism. This may be because of the smallness of the depicted figures.

Filigree art, in which artists weave and set very thin threads of silver or gold to make ornamental objects, is another big tradition in Turkey. This skill results in beautiful and intricate bracelets, rings and earrings, necklaces, prayer beads, brooches, belts, tobacco cases, and jewelry boxes.

Many more arts and crafts enrich the lives of the Turks. Among them are stained-glass production, marbling and gilding in book binding, wood engraving, calligraphy or hand lettering, fashion designing and couture, and *repoussé,* or designs inlaid into a surface. The centuries of beautiful artworks have left a legacy that today's artists and craftspeople cherish.

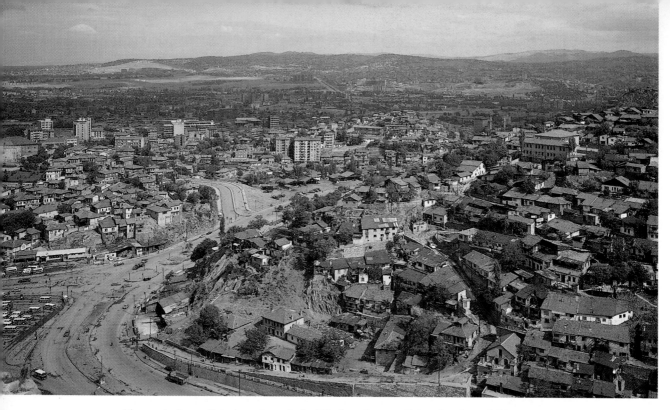

Above: Ankara, the newest capital of Turkey, has traditional red-roofed housing.
Below: Bodrum on the Aegean Sea is part of the Mediterranean sailing scene.

Chapter 8

CITIES AND PLACES

Most visitors, when they come to Turkey for the first time, "see" or "do" Istanbul and leave thinking that they know the country. Istanbul is a gigantic melting pot of races and customs, of the new and the old, and it does, of course, offer a lot to see. However, one must remember that the Turks came to Istanbul as late as the fifteenth century, while Anatolia or Asia Minor to the south, comprising 97 percent of Turkey's territory, had been occupied by either Turkic or much older civilizations since the start of recorded history.

ANKARA

Ankara deserves first mention because of its size—almost three million inhabitants—as well as for the fact that it is the capital of the country. Ankara's growth from a small city in the early twentieth century to its present status is perhaps unequaled among capital cities of the Old World. It may have been a small city as compared to Istanbul at the birth of the republic, but it was at least as old, if not older. The site of Ankara, in the northern section of the central Anatolian Plateau, was inhabited by settled peoples at least since the Stone Age. There are remains dating back

Left: Ataturk's Mausoleum and a museum in his honor are in Ankara.
Above: The Old Town of Ankara was built before the city became the capital of Turkey. It is surrounded by the newer city.

four thousand years, and a Phrygian town prospered in the area soon after that. Phrygians were ancient people of Thracian origin who had succeeded the Hittites, who built an empire in Anatolia from about 1450 to 1200 B.C., in controlling central Asia Minor.

Legend claims that the name *Ankara* came from an Egyptian anchor of the third century B.C. found by new settlers to the area. More probably, the name comes from a Phrygian word meaning "gorge" or "ravine." In the West, the name was Europeanized to "Angora," associated with the famous mohair wool produced by the long-haired goats of the region, and with the equally long-haired cats that go by that name.

As a thriving town in the path of traders and invaders, Ankara fell prey to Alexander the Great's Macedonians, Romans from Byzantium, Persians, Arabs, Seljuks, and Ottomans at different times in its rich and long history. It also played a key role in Turkey's War of Independence against Greece as headquarters for the resistance forces. These two facts moved Ataturk in 1923 to select Ankara as the republic's new capital.

Ankara has a relatively small hub of old, narrow streets and mud houses built on the slopes of a hill topped by a citadel or walled center, called the Ulus. There is a vast growth of modern buildings and housing extending mostly to the southwest. In the other directions, the city is surrounded by mountain ranges.

Ankara is a lively, modern capital offering much cultural activity, including a symphony orchestra, operatic and theatrical productions, various highly renowned annual festivals, and some of the richest museum collections in the country. Its Festival of Music and the Arts and its International Children's Festival are both held in April. Ataturk's tomb and a museum dedicated to his memory, both part of a monumental complex of simple, stark beauty, also are located in Ankara. This complex, known as the Ataturk Mausoleum, spreads out over a bluff commanding a breathtakingview of the modern part of the city.

IZMIR

Izmir, or Smyrna, as it used to be known in the West, vies in antiquity with Ankara, Istanbul, and other traditional parts of the country. It is Turkey's second-largest port and a close third to Ankara in population. But it is known primarily for industry and trade, rather than administration and services as is the case with Ankara. Izmir is the economic center of the region adjacent to the Aegean Sea and a leader in the production of woolen textiles, foodstuffs, and chemical and engineering works. It is Turkey's main shipping point for such agricultural specialties as tobacco,

Izmir is home to international trade fairs (left), while the surrounding terraced land is often used to grow grapes for wine (above).

figs, cotton, and vegetable produce.

Izmir's history goes back at least five thousand years. The old city center abounds with testimonies to its rich past, and it is said to rival even that of Athens, Greece, among the great Mediterranean cities. Izmir caters to the traditional tastes of the Turks, with its many coffee and teahouses, bars and public bathhouses, and bazaars and tiny shopping streets. But less traditional tastes are catered to, also, with theaters, international festivals and trade fairs, and nightlife. The deeply indented Aegean coastline, which extends north and southwest from Izmir, is lined with attractive beaches and resorts, making pleasure boating an industry.

The whole region is rich in archeological remains with unique treasures to be visited in the general area. To the north are the

ancient cities of Troy and Bergama (Pergamum), where parchment or goat skins used for writing and bookmaking is supposed to have originated. The biblical cities of Ephesus and Miletus are to the south.

ADANA

Adana is Turkey's fourth-largest city and the key to the plain of Cilicia. It lies at the foot of passes through the Taurus Mountains in southern Turkey. Adana was an important Hittite settlement as early as 1400 B.C. It was conquered by Alexander the Great in 335 B.C. and then changed hands over the centuries. Adana was often razed by its conquerors, and so conserves relatively few remnants of its rich past. Many historic monuments of Roman/Byzantine times are located in nearby sites such as Tarsus (where Saint Paul the Apostle was born) and Iskenderun, which is also known as *Alexandretta,* or Alexander's little city. Also near is Mersin, Adana's port and the center of an important complex of tourist areas well known for beautiful beaches and archeological remains of great antiquity.

Adana's prosperity today lies in its being the commercial center for the rich agricultural region of the Cilician Plain and Turkey's most important textile industry complex. The city has a great covered bazaar, many old mosques, and several important museums. Many well-preserved churches and other testimonials to the early Christian faith can also be found.

ANTAKYA AND THE TURKISH RIVIERA

Close to the easternmost point of Turkey's Mediterranean coastline lies Antakya (Antioch in the Bible). Conquered by Alexander and his Macedonian armies, it became the capital of the Seleucid kings, a dynasty started by one of Alexander's generals upon Alexander's death. Later it was a prized Roman colony.

During the early days of Christianity, Antioch was a center of religious activity. The apostles Peter and Paul visited the city and, just outside the urban center, Saint Peter's Grotto can still be visited. This is the name given today to a church built inside the cave where the Christian apostles preached jointly for the first time and established a Christian community.

Modern Antakya has countless remains from Roman times and many museums exhibiting priceless collections of centuries-old art and utility objects. Outstanding among them is the Hatay Museum, endowed with one of the world's richest collections of Roman mosaics or decorative tile work.

A long, softly curving coastline, by comparison to the abruptly indented Aegean coastline to the northwest, extends westward

The western end of the Turkish Riviera features great beauty, such as a sunken city (above) near Kas, and the ruins of the Greek stadium of Aspendos (right).

from Antakya to Antalya and is popularly known as the Turkish Riviera. It has endless beaches and resorts as well as numerous sites of matchless natural beauty and archeological complexes of interest to scholars and tourists alike.

BLACK SEA COASTLINE

If anybody ever thought of Turkey as a country of arid plains and barren mountain ranges, the sight of the Black Sea area would banish the idea. The whole northern sector of the country is a lush green quilt of rolling, or even mountainous, countryside covered with pine trees, meadows, and quaint villages, bordered by soft, enticing beaches caressed by the Black Sea and its temperate climate.

It is here one finds traditional Turkish residential architecture at its best. In the small town of Safranbolu, there are spacious

The hills overlooking the Black Sea town of Trabzon feature several monasteries and convents in startling locations.

three-storied, tile-roofed houses perched on the lush slopes of the Koroglu Mountains. The fertile, humid slopes of this region account as well for the richest and best tea and tobacco crops, most prized hazelnuts, most varied flowers, and choicest woods.

Another unique town, this one right on the coast, is Amasra, known as Sesamos in antiquity, and best known today for its simple beauty and its variety of water sports. Kastamonu, an inland town also abounding in Byzantine monuments, is particularly famous today for the richness of its wooden ceilings and panelings. Wood carving is still popular, and visitors often carry off samples of the local craftsmen's prized art.

Sinop is a natural port on the Black Sea. Its beaches are endless and unspoiled, and it is popular with boating fans. It also is an

The gently rolling farmland along the Black Sea coast may have Islamic mosques tucked into small valleys.

important fishing and shipping center for the area. Sinop has a beautiful castle-citadel dating back to the third century B.C. It was the birthplace of the philosopher Diogenes, who is reputed to have gone around with a lighted lantern even in broad daylight, endlessly searching for an honest man. Sinop's museum exhibits beautiful gold-inlaid Christian icons of past centuries.

The coastal town of Giresun and nearby Giresun Island are, locals claim, where the legendary Amazons, a nation of beautiful women warriors, settled in prehistory and lashed out at the surrounding territories. It was also from here that the Roman general Lucullus, famed for his conquests as well as for his luxurious tastes, exported cherries to Europe for the first time.

Perhaps the most important town of the easternmost part of the region, and most representative as well, is Trabzon (or Trebizond), a beautiful port city founded by ancient Greeks from Miletus. Two thousand years later, it became the Byzantine capital when Constantinople fell to the crusaders. But even after Constantinople

Beautiful Mount Erciyes, an extinct volcano at Kayseri in Central Anatolia, is almost 4,000 feet (1,219 meters) high.

was recovered, Trabzon remained as capital city to an offshoot empire known as the Comneni Dynasty, until the Ottomans captured it in 1461. The town and surroundings are rich in Byzantine churches and remains, where splendid Christian frescoes (paintings on walls) have been preserved.

The area is also well known for its beautiful lakes, many rivers and waterfalls, spas of thermal and medicinal waters, and general appeal to hikers, architecture buffs, skiers, and whitewater rafters.

CENTRAL ANATOLIA

Turkey's amazing variety, both topographically and culturally, is most evident in the vast interior of Asia Minor, or Anatolia.

Hattusas, east of Ankara, was the capital of the Hittite empire that controlled Anatolia from about 3,600 years ago. The Hittites were probably the first people to smelt iron.

Toward the west, it extends as a plateau, reminiscent of a beautiful Turkish carpet, fringed by mountains north and south and descending to the soft plains licked by the Aegean Sea. To the east, the plateau gradually tilts upward, and two parallel ranges (the Black Sea Mountains to the north and the Taurus Mountains to the south) merge into a towering mountainous mass that fills out most of Turkey's eastern portion. The rest consists of a flat triangle to the southeast roughly contained between the historic Euphrates and Tigris River basins.

Ankara lies close to the center of the western portion of Turkey's inlands, known as the Central Plateau. This plateau, with its characteristic burnt-ocher color, mixed with greens of every

Sunflowers grow in the lava-based soil of Cappadocia.

hue, is majestic in its vastness and its frequent patches of emptiness. This is where some of the earliest civilizations known to man have arisen and, in some places, archeological remains of settlements dating back as far as eight thousand years B.C. have been discovered.

West of Ankara lies Gordion, a town that for centuries served as capital to the Phrygians, whose king was Gordius. The legend of Alexander the Great states it was here that the young conqueror came upon the Gordian knot, a knot so intricate that it could be undone only by the man who could conquer the world beyond it. Alexander, unawed, simply cut the knot with a quick stroke of his sword, and went on to invade and conquer the rest of known Asia.

To the north of Ankara lie many historic cities and towns. One of them, Cankiri, boasts an eleventh-century Seljuk castle that dominates the town and a mosque built by Sinan, the Ottoman

For centuries, Christians lived in homes and worshiped in chapels that they carved out of the volcanic rock, called tufa, found in the rugged landscape of Cappadocia. At Goreme, an important open-air museum preserves such places.

architect. One of the best skiing areas in Turkey can be found nearby at Ilgaz. A bit farther east, set into a river canyon, is Amasya, which some claim to be the most beautiful town in Turkey. High above its residential sectors, carved into the rocky cliffs overhanging the city, are impressive Roman tombs and a Seljuk citadel with a lavish Ottoman palace inside it. Amasya's old wooden houses and palaces have been restored and today some are inns, museums, or art galleries. The surrounding countryside is rich in lakes, forests, and patches of vines bearing a delicious deep-red variety of grape.

Especially noteworthy on the southeast sector of the plateau is the area known today as the Goreme, or by its old Latin name, the Cappadocia. The Goreme is one of those odd marvels where humans and nature have made something unique. Approximately three million years ago, two volcanoes of the area, Mount Erciyes and Mount Hasan, erupted and covered their surroundings with lava, ashes, and clay. Through the ages, winds and rain eroded the hardened material in such a way that it has today become a spectacular and surrealistic landscape dotted with improbable-looking chimneys or cones. These were burrowed into by generations of ancient cave dwellers. Early Christians used them to celebrate their rituals or to hide from Persian, Arabic, or Mongol pursuers. Today they are part of open-air museums and, in some cases, are used as restaurants and art galleries.

Equally amazing are the formations at Pamukkale to the southwest. *Pamukkale* means "cotton castle," a name given the region because streams fed with calcium-rich waters have solidified into superimposed pools that look like frozen white confectionery.

Other important towns on this plateau and to the northeast of Ankara are Tokat, with numerous Seljuk and Ottoman monuments, and Zile, where Julius Caesar allegedly uttered his famous phrase, "*Veni, vidi, vici,*" meaning "I came, I saw, I conquered." Nearby Sivas contains Seljuk constructions of several theological schools, a school of medicine, and a hospital that show the standards of civilization already attained by the twelfth and thirteenth centuries. Sivas is also known for its rugs.

Almost straight to the south from Ankara lies Konya, one of the country's oldest continuously inhabited centers. Known as Iconium by the Romans, it later served as the Seljuk capital during the twelfth and thirteenth centuries A.D. It was here that a Muslim Sufi mystic called Mevlana founded his order of the dervishes, known popularly as the "whirling dervishes." In today's seminary adjoining Mevlana's Mausoleum, the dervishes still perform, purportedly in a trance induced by their whirling and flowing motions. Konya also has many Seljuk monuments, including the great Aladdin Mosque built by Sultan Aladdin Keykubat in the early thirteenth century and several Islamic theological schools. Its museum collections are renowned.

This farm woman is spreading corn (maize) to dry in the bright eastern Anatolian sunshine.

EASTERN ANATOLIA

The eastern half of Anatolia is mostly rugged country, the plateau itself tilting upward toward the rising sun and reaching levels of 6,000 to 7,000 feet (1,829 to 2,134 meters) close to the Russian and Iranian borders. This area's key city is Erzurum, a treasure trove of Seljuk architecture. Its Byzantine fortress walls and some masterful Ottoman mosques, such as one by the famous architect Sinan, are also noteworthy. Kars is another historic city, which contains frequent elements of Russian influence in its architecture. Kars is particularly famed for its *kilims,* or reversible prayer rugs and carpets. The ski slopes nearby are popular.

A little to the south one finds the towns of Igdir, Agri, and Dogubuyazit, all related one way or another to the towering Mount Ararat of Biblical fame located in the area. Agri (Ararat) takes its name from the mountain rising to 17,011 feet (5,185

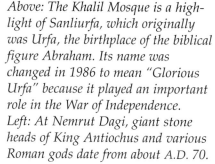

Above: The Khalil Mosque is a high-light of Sanliurfa, which originally was Urfa, the birthplace of the biblical figure Abraham. Its name was changed in 1986 to mean "Glorious Urfa" because it played an important role in the War of Independence.
Left: At Nemrut Dagi, giant stone heads of King Antiochus and various Roman gods date from about A.D. 70.

meters), on whose slopes it is perched. Igdir lies in a fertile valley to which, by tradition, Noah and his family descended after the Great Flood. And it is said that near Dogubuyazit Noah's wife prepared a special dish with food remaining after the Ark finally touched down on the slopes of Mount Ararat. That tasty dessert known as Noah's Pudding is still prepared locally.

To the south, a wide triangle of flat land known as the Upper Mesopotamian Plain opens up. It is roughly contained between the

Ruins of an ancient fortress overlook Lake Van in eastern Anatolia. It is a salt-water lake almost 1,500 square miles (3,885 square kilometers) in area.

river basins of the Tigris and the Euphrates. This area is the cradle of one of the oldest known civilizations. Around Gaziantep to the west, the plain is fertile and green, with plentiful crops of olives, wine grapes, and pistachio nuts. Gaziantep itself is built around a citadel with thirty-six lofty towers, first erected by the Byzantines in Justinian's time, then destroyed and rebuilt by the Seljuks. Gaziantep's artisans specialize in copper and brass handiwork and furniture rich in mother-of-pearl inlay. The town's cooks are known for their delicious brand of baklavah.

Toward the center of the Upper Mesopotamian Plain, and close to the border with Syria, stands Sanliurfa, a city of extreme antiquity believed to have been a Sumerian regional center several thousand years ago. According to tradition, Abraham was born in a cave next to where the city's great mosque of Mevlid Halil stands today. The city harbors one of Turkey's best archeological and ethnographic museums. Also on this barren plain stands Harran, a city mentioned in the Bible's Book of Genesis as that in which Abraham resided, and better known today for its beehive-shaped mud dwellings.

With a seven-decade history of democracy, Turks decide their future in elections; shown above is Trabzon at election time. Economically, Turkey is overcoming its problems; the engineers at the left are working in Seydisehir.

THE FUTURE

Clearly, amazing diversity is the essence of this wonderful country. This is so for its geography as well as its ancient and present-day cultures. However, one can only venture an uncertain and worried guess as to its future. Turkey indeed has problems, and important ones, too. One is the energy-draining Kurdish problem with its frightening terrorism and its moral implications. The Muslim fundamentalist revival, which threatens to do away with the rights of half of Turkey's population (women) while endeavoring to recover a simpler, more spiritual way of life, is another. Also, there is a concern about the nation's economic and political problems, although they may, in fact, be easier to solve than the religious or ethnic ones.

Kurdish civilians take cover during a battle between the Turkish army troops and Kurdish guerrillas. Solving the problem of the Kurds will be an important issue throughout the region.

But Turks are a brave and dynamic people. They have progressed in the new republic barely seven decades old and have retained their honest, sturdy pride, their happy style of life, and their deep sense of family strength and responsibility.

There is a Turkish proverb that says: "The arrow has left the bow." Western cultures have it, too. We say, "The die is cast" or "We've burned our bridges behind us," as ways of expressing a sense of resolution. Turks feel bound to such a sense and, even more so, to their conception of fate. Turkey opted for democracy, progress, and Westernization under the leadership of one great statesman, Ataturk, and the point of no return was reached quickly. Traditions will be kept, enriching the life of the nation, and controversy will not die down. But perhaps such conflict is the essence of democracy. Turkey will press forward, because the arrow has left the bow.

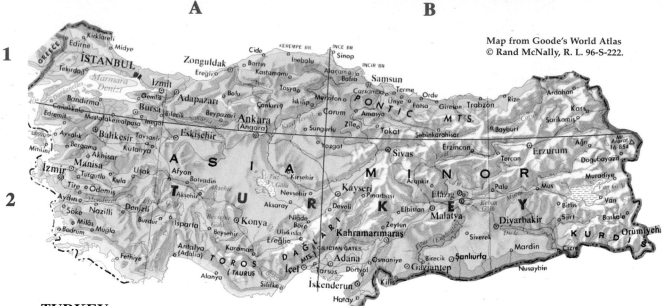

Map from Goode's World Atlas
© Rand McNally, R. L. 96-S-222.

TURKEY

Adana	2B	Bodrum	2A	Gaziantep	2B	Merzifon	1B	Sungurlu	1A
Adapazan	1A	Bolu	1A	Gemlik	1A	Midye	1A	Tarsus	2A
Afyon	2A	Bolvadin	2A	Giresun	1B	Milas	2A	Taurus Mts. (Oros	
Agri	2B	Bor	2A	Hatay	2B	Mt. Ararat	2B	Daglari)	2A
Akhisar	2A	Burdur	2A	Icel	2A	Mugla	2A	Tavsanli	2A
Aksaray	2A	Bursa	1A	Inebolu	1A	Muradiye	2B	Tekirdag	1A
Aksehir	2A	Canakkale	1A	Inegol	1A	Mus	2B	Tercan	2B
Aksehir (lake)	2A	Cankiri	1A	Iskenderun	2B	Mustafake-		Terme	1B
Alacam	1B	Carsamba	1B	Iskilip	1A	malpasa	1A	Tire	2A
Alanya	2A	Cide	1A	Isparta	2A	Nazilli	2A	Tokar	1B
Amasya	1B	Cilician Gates	2B	Istanbul	1A	Nevsehir	2A	Tosya	1A
Ankara	2A	Cizre	2B	Izmir	2A	Nigde	2A	Trabzon	1B
Antalya	2A	Corum	1A	Izmit	1A	Nusaybin	2B	Turgutlu	2A
Arapkir	2B	Denizli	2A	Kahramari-		Odemis	2A	Tuz Golu	
Ardahan	1B	Develi	2B	maras	2B	Ordu	1B	(lake)	2A
Aydino	2A	Diyarbakir	2B	Karaman	2A	Osmaniye	2B	Ulakisla	2A
Ayvalik	2A	Dogubuyazit	2B	Kars	1B	Palu	2B	Unye	1B
Bafra	1B	Dortyol	2B	Kastamonu	1A	Pinarbasi	2B	Usak	2A
Balikesir	2A	Edirne	1A	Kayseri	2B	Pontic Mts.	1B	Van	2B
Bandirma	1A	Edremit	2A	Keban Golu		Rize	1B	Van Golu	2B
Bartin	1A	Egridir Golu		(lake)	2B	Samsun	1B	Yozgat	2A
Baskale	2B	(lake)	2A	Kilis	2B	Sanliurfa	2B	Zeytun	2B
Bayburt	1B	Elazig	2B	Kirklareli	1A	Sarikamis	1B	Zile	1B
Bergama	2A	Elbistan	2B	Kirsehir	2A	Sebinkara-		Zonguldak	1A
Beypazari	1A	Eregli	1A	Konya	2A	hisar	1B		
Beysehir	2A	Eregli	2A	Kula	2A	Siirt	2B		
Beysehir Golu		Erzincan	2B	Kurdistan	2B	Silifke	2A		
(lake)	2A	Erzurum	2B	Kutahya	2A	Sinop	1B		
Bilecik	1A	Eskisehir	2A	Malatya	2B	Sivas	2B		
Birecik	2B	Fatsa	1B	Manisa	2A	Siverek	2B		
Bitlis	2B	Fethiye	2A	Mardin	2B	Soke	2A		

112

MINI-FACTS AT A GLANCE

GENERAL INFORMATION

Official Name: Turkiye Cumhuriyeti (Republic of Turkey).

Capital: Ankara.

Government: Turkey is a multiparty parliamentary republic with one legislative house—the Turkish Grand National Assembly. Chief of government is the prime minister who is also head of the Council of Ministers. The president is the head of the state and is elected by the Grand National Assembly for a seven-year term. The president selects the prime minister from the majority party in the legislature. General elections are held every five years. The highest court of appeal is the Constitution Court. Turkey's most prominent political parties are the Welfare Party, the Motherland, the True Path, the Social Democratic Populist Party, and the National Democracy Party.

For administrative purposes, the country is divided into 76 provinces, which are further divided into counties, districts, municipalities, and villages.

Religion: Turkey is a secular country. The constitution guarantees religious freedom to all. More than 98 percent of the Turkish population follows Islam, mostly of the Sunni branch. Small Christian and Jewish communities are concentrated in the larger cities.

Ethnic Composition: About 85 percent of the population belongs to the Turkic ethnic group. Minor ethnic groups are the Kurds, Arabs, Caucasians, Greeks, Jews, and Armenians.

Language: The country's official language is Turkish. Almost all (about 95 percent) Turkish people speak the Turkish language. Since 1923 Turkish has been written in the Latin script instead of in the Arabic script. Kurdish is spoken by some 6 percent of the population, mostly in eastern and southeastern Anatolia. Arabic, Greek, and Armenian are spoken by small numbers of people, mostly in the larger cities.

National Flag: Adopted in 1936, the Turkish flag consists of traditional Islamic symbols, a crescent moon and a five-pointed star, in white over a red background. Red is the color of the Ottoman Empire that introduced Islam in Turkey.

National Emblem: An elliptical red shield bears the name of the Turkish Republic in Turkish in gold letters at the top; the traditional Islamic symbols of a crescent moon and a five-pointed star in white are in the center of the shield.

National Anthem: *"Korkma! Sonmez bu safaklarda yuzen al sancak"* ("Be not afraid! Our flag will never fade").

National Calendar: The Gregorian calendar is in use. The Western solar calendar is used for all nonreligious purposes, and the Islamic lunar calendar is used for religious purposes.

Money: Turkish lira (LT) is the official currency. In October 1996, 91,848 Turkish lira were worth one U.S. dollar.

Membership in International Organizations: Asian Development Bank (AsDB); Black Sea Economic Co-operation Group; General Agreement on Tariffs and Trade (GATT); Economic Cooperation Organization (EOC); North Atlantic Treaty Organization (NATO); Organization for Economic Cooperation and Development (OECD); International Bank for Reconstruction and Development ("World Bank"); United Nations (UN).

Weights and Measures: The metric system is in use.

Population: 63,204,000 (1996 estimate); with a density of 211 per sq. mi. (82 per sq km); 60 percent live in cities, and 40 percent are rural.

Cities:

Istanbul	7,331,927
Ankara	2,719,981
Izmir	1,920,807
Adana	1,010,363
Bursa	949,810
Gaziantep	683,557
Konya	558,308

(Based on 1993 population estimates)

GEOGRAPHY

Border: Turkey is bordered by both land and water on all four sides. The Black Sea is to the north, the Mediterranean Sea to the southwest, and the Aegean Sea to the west. The Sea of Marmara connects the Black Sea (through the Bosporus Strait) and the Mediterranean Sea (through the Dardanelles Channel). Greece and Bulgaria lie to the west, Syria and Iraq to the south, Iran and Armenia to the east, and Georgia to the north.

Coastline: 2,211 mi. (3,558 km).

Land: Some 3 percent of Turkey is located in the continent of Europe, and the rest is in Asia. The Asian portion occupies the whole Anatolian Peninsula. Turkey's varied topography includes rugged mountain ranges in the west and south, high plateaus in the central area, and a mixture of river plains and lake country in the east. The arid and steppe-like Anatolian Plateau has cold winters and low rainfall, and periodically experiences severe droughts. The Eastern Highlands, covering one-third of the country, have very little population; there are about a hundred peaks with elevations of 10,000 feet (3,000 m) or more. The Bursa Plains near the Aegean Sea coast are heavily populated.

The Pontic Mountains stretch in the north along the Black Sea coast. The Taurus and the AntiTaurus Mountains are in the south. Hilly slopes suffer from serious soil erosion. Turkey lies in an unstable region that is prone to earthquakes.

Highest Point: Mount Ararat, 17,011 ft. (5,185 m).

Lowest Point: At sea level along the coast.

Rivers: The Euphrates and the Tigris Rivers originate in the Eastern Highlands region and flow south into Iraq. The Kizil Irmak is the longest river in Turkey (60 mi. ; 96 km); it flows into the Black Sea. Most Turkish rivers are not suitable for navigation purposes because of the seasonal variation in water flow, but they are good sources of hydroelectricity. Most of the seasonal rivers dry up in the long hot summers. Turkey has several saltwater lakes. Lake Tuz is an important source of salt, as the salt content in its water is very high; it also dries up in the long harsh summers. Lake Van, also salty, is in the southeast.

Forests: Some 40 percent of Turkey is under rich and productive forests, which yield wood not only for export, but also for use in local construction, furniture, and paper industries. Oak, wild olive, and licorice trees grow in the southwest.

Wildlife: Turkey's fauna include deer, wild boar, hare, leopard, brown bear, red fox, gazelle, wildcat, lynx, otter, snakes, and badger. Birds are plentiful including snow partridge, quail, bustard, woodcock, and many species of geese, ducks, and pigeons.

Climate: Turkey's climate is moderated by the Mediterranean Sea in the southwest and by the Black Sea in the north. The southwest has mild, rainy winters and hot, dry summers with temperatures higher than 90° F. (32° C) in the summer. Northeastern Turkey has mild summers but very cold winters with temperatures as low as –40° F. (–40° C). The Central Anatolian Plateau has cold winters and some snowstorms. Annual rainfall varies from 20 to 30 inches (50 to 75 cm) along the Mediterranean coast to more than 100 inches (255 cm) near the Black Sea. Most of the Anatolia Plateau is dry throughout the year.

Greatest Distance: North to South: 465 mi. (748 km).
                          East to West: 1,015 mi. (1,633 km).

Area: 301,382 sq. mi. (780,576 sq km).

ECONOMY AND INDUSTRY

Agriculture: The most productive farmlands are in the coastal region where soil is fertile. Agriculture employs some 60 percent of the population. Turkey is a world leader in the production of cereals, wheat, barley, maize (corn), lentils, eggplants, chickpeas, and beans. Turkey is self-sufficient in most of the basic foodstuffs. Major commercial crops are sugar beets, tea leaves, coffee beans, cotton, and tobacco. Turkey produces a variety of fruits and vegetables such as apples, grapes, figs, and hazelnuts. Cultivation of opium poppies is restricted. Livestock products include milk, wool, poultry, and eggs. Very delicate, fine, and warm mohair wool is produced by Angora (originally: Ankara) goats. Long-haired cats are also called Angoras. Silkworms and bees are cultivated.

Turkey produces vegetable oils such as olive, cotton, sunflower, and peanut oils for both commercial and local use. Fisheries contribute significantly to the economy; anchovies, mackerel, sardines, and bluefish are the most common fish caught.

Mining: Turkey has significant resources of granite, marble, magnesite, boron salts, barite, chromium, copper, iron, thorium (70 percent of the world's reserve), hard coal, lignite, asphaltite, tungsten, crude oil, nickel, and manganese. Turkey is one of the largest producers of boron salt, which is used in the chemical industries. Lignite coal is used to produce electricity.

Manufacturing: Turkey's industrial output includes petroleum and petro-chemical byproducts, consumer goods (processed foods, fabric, clothing, leather goods, beverages, furniture, shoes, and tobacco products), iron and steel, plastics, cement, and glass. Other industries such as motor vehicles, metalware, electronics, heavy machinery, and agricultural equipment are gaining importance.

Tourism: Tourism has emerged as a major service industry in the last few decades; it has become one of the largest sources of foreign exchange. Turkey's treasure of architectural monuments and historic remains draw a large number of foreign visitors. The Turkish tourism authority promotes mountaineering, thermal spas, whitewater rafting, fishing, and hunting. The Turkish Riviera has numerous beaches and resorts mixed with natural beauty. Some of the best skiing areas in Turkey are near Ilgaz.

Transportation: In 1993 the total length of railroads was 6,470 mi. (10,413 km), which is very small for a country of Turkey's size. Total length of the roads was 240,286 mi. (386,704 km), of which about 15 percent are paved. Almost all towns are connected by the road system; buses, trains, and taxis are the most commonly used modes of transportation. The national airlines, the government-owned Turkish Airlines, serves many cities in Europe and the Middle East. International airports serve Ankara and Istanbul. Turkey's long coastline has several good harbors; Istanbul is the largest seaport, followed by Izmir, Samsun, and Mersin.

Communication: There are about 31 daily newspapers, mostly in the cities of Istanbul, Ankara, and Izmir. In the early 1990s, there was one radio receiver for seven persons, one television for six persons, and one telephone for five persons.

Trade: Chief imports are machinery, petroleum, iron and steel, motor vehicles, and electrical and electronic equipment. Major import sources are Germany, the United States, Italy, Russia, France, and Saudi Arabia. Chief export items are textiles, iron and steel products, fruits, and machinery. Major export destinations are Germany, the United States, Russia, Italy, United Kingdom, and France.

EVERYDAY LIFE

Health: Health standards in Turkey are generally good. Life expectancy at 69 years for males and 73 years for females is high compared to other Asian countries. An infant mortality rate of 49 per 1,000 is high. In the mid-1990s, there were about 1,100 persons per physician, and about 420 persons per hospital bed.

Education: Education is universal and compulsory at the primary and intermediate levels (ages 6 to 14). Tuition is free in public schools all the way to the university level; coeducation is promoted by the government. Secondary education begins at the age of 11 and lasts for up to six years. Schools are closed on Saturday and Sunday, and vacations are in the summer. Technical training schools provide vocational education. Higher education is conducted by more than fifty public and private universities. Many higher learning institutes conduct research in the fields of health, solar energy, marine science, ecology, biomedicine, television, and cinema. In the early 1990s, the literacy rate was about 83 percent. Government spends some 10 percent of its budget on providing and enhancing educational facilities, especially in the rural areas.

Holidays:
>   New Year's Day, January 1
>   National Sovereignty and Children's Day, April 23
>   Commemoration of Ataturk and Youth and Sports Day, May 19
>   Victory Day, August 30
>   Republic Day, October 29

Some holidays, such as the Feast of the Sacrifice and the End of Ramadan, are based on the Islamic lunar calendar and may vary by a few days every year.

Culture: Turkish culture is a mixture of old and new traditions, and Islamic and nonreligious traditions. Istanbul was known in the ancient times as Constantinople and Byzantium. Istanbul is spread on the continents of Asia and Europe, and is one of the world's major melting pots of races and cultures. The city's antique section is known as Stamboul and its relatively modern sections as Beyoglu and Uskudar. The Topkapi Palace in Istanbul houses invaluable art, jewels, and furniture from the past. There are many art galleries and close to 500 museums. The Archaeological Museum, the Turkish and Islamic Art Museum, and the Painting and Sculpture Museum are in Istanbul.

Turkey's whirling dervishes belong to a mystical order of Islamic monks of the Sufi branch; they express their belief in the purity and peace of one's heart through religious dancing.

Society: Slavery was abolished in the mid-nineteenth century. After Turkey became a republic in 1923, equal rights were guaranteed to all citizens. Turkish women's status changed rapidly during the 1920s when government outlawed the marriage contract system and made it easier for women to obtain divorce. They were given the right to vote and to receive alimony. Turkish women are at a par with men in every sense. They are not required to wear restrictive dress, and they enjoy equal opportunities for education, inheritance, and equal pay for identical jobs. Women are journalists, business leaders, educators, and political leaders. However, in rural areas, the father is the undisputed head of the family.

Several government and private organizations promote youth activities. Youth groups and centers are well organized, and young people are encouraged to participate in traditional folk dancing, folk music, and social events.

Handicrafts: The weaving of carpets and prayer rugs is one of the most important traditional handicrafts of the Turkish people. As Islam forbids the depiction of human figures, carpet weavers have developed their own unique subjects such as stars, polygons, and other geometric figures. Turkish carpets are known for the complexity of subjects and rare depth of color. These rugs are made out of cotton, wool, or silk. The silk carpets can have hundreds of knots per square inch. Miniature painting and embroidered pieces are traditional gift items. Filigree art is used to make beautiful bracelets, rings, earrings, necklaces, prayer beads, brooches, belts, tobacco cases, and jewelry boxes. Stained-glass production, book binding, wood engraving, and calligraphy are very popular.

Dress: Turkish clothing underwent dramatic changes in the 1920s. Urban people largely adopted the Western style of clothing. Traditional Islamic dress of a loose-fitting cloak and loose trousers for men is still popular in the villages. Women's traditional dress consists of loose-fitting pantaloons and long blouses. Rural women generally cover their head and the lower part of the chin by a scarf. Wearing of the concealing veil by women was outlawed in the 1920s.

Housing: Turkish housing style and materials vary from region to region. In the Black Sea region, housing is chiefly of thatched roofs and wooden structure. In the northeast, mud and wooden houses have been largely replaced by concrete houses. Flat-roofed houses of either stone or dried-mud bricks are common in the rural areas. Wealthy Turks live in spacious concrete-block homes in the suburbs of cities. The government has been constructing mass apartment complexes, especially in the big cities, to relieve housing shortages.

Food: Wheat-bread and yogurt are the staples of the Turkish diet. Lamb, rice, and eggplant are also popular food items. Special Turkish foods are rice or *pilaf* dishes with chunks of lamb or shrimp or other seafood. *Imambayildi* is a popular eggplant dish; stuffed vegetables in cabbage leaves are traditional favorites. Desserts include Turkish rice pudding, *samsa* (pastry with walnuts), *baklavah* (flaky pastry with honey), and "Turkish delights." Turkish tea and thick coffee, sweetened with sugar, are world famous. Aniseed-flavored *raki* is the most famous Turkish wine.

Sports and Recreation: Football (American soccer) is the most popular sport. People also enjoy archery, basketball, wrestling, weight lifting, fencing, handball, horseback riding, karate, judo, table tennis, shooting, volleyball, skiing, yachting, and scuba diving. Grease wrestling is a unique Turkish sport.

Turkish people enjoy drinking coffee or tea in small roadside cafes, and spend a good amount of recreation time in these coffee houses with their friends. Playing games of dice is a favorite leisure activity. Turkish music has strong Arab and Persian influences.

Kurdish Autonomy: The Kurdish problem in southern Turkey and adjoining areas of Iraq and Iran is a very complex issue. The Kurds, an ethnic minority, have long lived in tribal groups in isolated communities in this region. The government's attempt to bring them into the mainstream has largely met with armed resistance. Kurds have been demanding autonomy and a separate state for themselves, and guerrilla fighting has been going on for several decades. Recently, a large number of Kurds have fled from Iraq, Iran, and Russia and taken refuge in Turkey.

IMPORTANT DATES

3,000 B.C. — The oldest of the eight versions of a settlement later identified with Troy is started.

800 B.C. — A Greek settlement is located at the present-day site of Uskudar.

6th century B.C. — Byzantium is founded.

512 B.C. — Byzantium falls to King Darius of Persia.

478 B.C. — Byzantium falls once again to the Persians.

A.D. 2nd century — Roman Emperor Septimus Severus razes Byzantium and massacres its inhabitants.

268 — Roman Emperor Gallienus ravages Byzantium once more.

324 — Constantine defeats his enemies and becomes head of the Roman Empire. He proclaims Byzantium as the New Rome and renames it Constantinople.

325 — The huge church (later a mosque) Hagia Sophia (or Santa Sophia) is built.

330 — The city of Constantinople is officially inaugurated on May 11.

5th century — Emperor Theodosius builds walls around Constantinople.

8th century — Islam, the religion taught by Muhammad, is introduced to the Turkish people.

1071 — The Byzantine forces are defeated by the Seljuk Turks at the Battle of Manzikert.

1203 — Armies of the Fourth Crusade lay siege to Constantinople, starting fifty-seven years of crusader rule.

1261 — Greek Emperor Michael VIII Paleologus takes over Constantinople from the crusaders.

1326 — The Ottoman Empire, the center of which is the eventual country of Turkey, begins.

1422 — The Ottoman Turks lay siege unsuccessfully to Constantinople.

1453 — The Ottoman Turks conquer Constantinople under Sultan Fatih Mehmet II; Emperor Constantine XI Paleologus is killed. The University of Istanbul is founded.

1826 — The conservative Janissaries' leaders are massacred in the Hippodrome during the rule of Sultan Mahmoud II.

1830 — Turkey loses Algeria (in northern Africa) to France.

1839 — Sultan Abdulmecid I grants rights to all citizens of Istanbul, regardless of religion.

1878 — Great Britain takes over Cyprus from Turkey.

1881 — France captures Tunisia from Turkey.

1908 — The Young Turk Movement, under the leadership of Mustafa Kemal (later Ataturk), deposes the ruling sultan.

1914 — Turkey enters World War I on the side of Germany and Austria-Hungary.

1918 — Turkey is defeated by the Allied forces in World War I; Greece occupies the country.

1922 — Turkey wins its War of Independence from Greece; all occupying Greek forces are withdrawn.

1923 — The Republic of Turkey is proclaimed; sweeping cultural and political reforms are undertaken; many traditional Islamic practices are outlawed; the capital is moved from Istanbul to Ankara.

1924 — The Turkish caliphate, or religious monarchy, is abolished.

1925 — Kurds revolt to gain autonomy.

1928 — Government introduces Latin script for writing modern Turkish; most foreign words are eliminated.

1939 — A destructive earthquake kills about 30,000 people in the Erzincan area.

1945 — Turkey joins the United Nations.

1947 — The United States provides aid to Turkey to fight the expansionist Communist policy of the Soviet Union.

1950 — The country's first free elections are held; the Democratic Party wins the absolute majority.

1960-61 — The military rules for a year until national elections are held in 1961.

1961 — Development and planning are made a mandatory constitutional requirement; a new constitution is adopted and the military withdraws from direct political control.

1968 — Television is introduced in Turkey.

1974 — Turkish forces invade the island of Cyprus as the Greek Cypriots agitate to merge Cyprus with Greece; Turkey occupies the northern third of Cyprus.

1980-83 — Turkey is once again under military rule; a civilian government is established in 1983.

1982 — A new constitution with liberal and forward-looking amendments comes into force.

1990 — Turkey sides with the United States-led coalition against Iraq in the Persian Gulf War; it closes the pipeline at Kirkuk as part of the UN sanctions against Iraq.

1993 — Tansu Ciller becomes Turkey's first woman prime minister.

1996 — Prime Minister Tansu Ciller resigns after losing elections to the fundamentalist Welfare Party, which lacks a straight majority. It agrees to govern in a coalition with Ciller's party under the prime ministry of moderate fundamentalist Necmettan Erbakan. Relations with Russia are strained as Turkey criticizes Russia's suppression of the separatist movement in Chechnya. Kurdish conflict escalates, resulting in hundreds of deaths. Istanbul hosts the second United Nations Conference on Human Settlement attended by some 170 nations.

IMPORTANT PEOPLE

Mustafa Kemal Pasha "Ataturk" (1881–1938), the great leader of modern Turkey; he is also known as the "Father of the Nation." Ataturk modernized the country, declared it a republic, and was the first president of the Republic. He believed in the policy of coexistence and nonexpansionism.

Celal Bayar (1883–1986), helped to form the Democratic Party and was president (1950–60).

Tansu Ciller (1946–), Turkey's first female prime minister from, 1993 to 1996; a former university professor of economics, she joined the True Path Party in 1990; she became its leader and then prime minister in 1993.

Constantine I, the Great (280–337), Roman emperor; a great leader, soldier, and administrator; he converted to Christianity and proclaimed total freedom of religious beliefs in the city of Constantinople.

Necmettan Erbakan, elected to head Turkey's coalition government after his fundamentalist Welfare Party's relative 1996 victory.

Muksin Ertugul, Turkey's most renowned film-maker of the twentieth century.

Fuzuli (1494–1555), a poet renowned for his lyrical verses.

Seyh Galib (1757–98), great Turkish poet of mystical and classical tradition.

Sultan Abdul Hamid II (1842–1918), a tyrannical ruler who was the sultan when the Young Turk Movement was formed.

Ismet Inonu (1884–1973), Turkish leader who was a friend and follower of Ataturk; he succeeded Kemal as president (1938–50).

Justinian I (483–565), a Byzantine emperor best known for his collection of written laws and legal principles.

Suna Konrad (1934–), classical soprano, well known outside Turkey, especially in Europe.

Sultan Fatih Mehmet II (1429–81), Ottoman sultan; he took over Constantinople in 1453, renamed it Istanbul, and made it his new capital; he converted most of the Christian churches to mosques.

Ahmet Nedim (1681–1730), one of the greatest poets of the Ottoman Turkey.

Turgut Ozal (1927 –1993); prime minister of Turkey from 1983 to 1989, and president from 1989 to 1993; He was also the founder of the Motherland Party.

Anwar Pasha (1881–1922), Young Turk leader, ruler of Turkey during World War I.

Ziya Pasha (1825–80), one of the outstanding literary figures of the reform period.

Mevlana Rurni (1207–73), the author of the epic *Mesnevi* and founder of the Mevlevi Dervishes, a religious sect popularly called "whirling dervishes."

Omer Seyfettin (1884–1920), an important short-story writer.

Mimar Sinan (16th century), Turkish architect who built some 300 buildings all over the Ottoman Empire during the reign of Suleyman the Magnificent.

Sinasi (1826–71), a dramatist, journalist, essayist, and writer.

Suleyman the Magnificent (1494–1566), Ottoman sultan from 1520 to 1566, also known as the Lawgiver; his empire stretched from Morocco in North Africa to Afghanistan in Asia, and from the Indian Ocean to Hungary in Europe.

Kemal Tahir, writer, wrote mostly about village life in realistic terms.

Haci Bektas Veli (1242–1337), founder of the Bektashi Dervishes, a religious sect.

Compiled by Chandrika Kaul, Ph.D.

INDEX

Page numbers that appear in **boldface type** indicate illustrations

The Abduction from the Seraglio 86
Abdul Hamid II, Sultan 37, 122
Abdulmecid I, Sultan 37, 120
Abraham 74, **78**, 108, 109
Abu Kabr 72
Adana 59, 97, 98, 114
Aegean islands 32, 98
Aegean Sea **6**, 8, 17, 18, 19, 103, 114, 115
Afghanistan 34, 122
Africa 12, 120
Agri 107
agricultural equipment 46, 51, 116
agriculture 46, **49**, 50, 53, 60, 96, 98, 115, 116
Ahmet Nedim 122
air travel 79, 116
Akkad 7
Aladdin Keykubat, Sultan 106
Aladdin Mosque 106
Alanya **6**, **12**
Albania 44
Alexander the Great 19, **23**, 94, 97, 98, 104
Alexandretta 97
Algeria 120
Ali 72
Allah 69, 71, 76, 77, 84
Allied Forces 38, 39, 48, 120
Alpine people 58
alternative energy sources 46, 51
Amasra 100
Amasya 105
Amazons 101
amendments 42, 121
amphitheaters **86**
Anatolia 13, 32, 45, 55, 56, 57, 81, 90, 93, 94, 102-109, 113, 115
Anatolian Civilizations Museum 89
Anatolian Peninsula 7, 11, 22, 45, 114
Anatolian Plateau 94, 114
Angora, see Ankara
Angora cats 94, 116
Angora goats 94, 116
animism 69
Ankara 21, 38, 43, **45**, **54**, 55, **56**, 59, 86, 87, 88, 89, 92, 93, **94**, 95, 103, 104, 106, 113, 114, 116, 120
Antakya 98, 99
Antalya 99

Antioch, see Antakya
Antiochus **108**
AntiTaurus Mountains 115
apartment complexes **59**, 118
Apostles 88
apples 50, 116
aqueduct **25**
Arabia 69, 73
Arabian Peninsula 69
Arabic **56**, 57, **78**, 106, 113
Arabs 28, 29, 44, 56, 58, 69, 84, 95, 113, 119
Ararat 107; see also Mount Ararat
Archangel Gabriel 71
archeological remains 53, 88, 89, 97, 98, 99, 104, 109, 117
archery 64, 119
architecture 26, 53, 75, 81, 82, 88, 99, 105, 107, 116, 122
Argo **18**
Argonauts 18
Armenia 8, 114
Armenians 57, 113
army 37, 111
art galleries 105, 106, 117
arts 26, 33, 66, **70**, 81, 82, 88, 89, 91, 98, 100, 106, 117
Asia **21**
Asia Minor 10, 74, 93, 94, 102
Asian Development Bank 114
Aspendos **99**
asphaltite 51, 116
Ataturk, see Kemal, Mustafa Pasha "Ataturk"
Ataturk Dam **46**
Ataturk Mausoleum 89, **94**, 95
Athens 23, 96
Attila **10**
Augusti emperors 24
Austria-Hungary 39, 120
Azerbaijan 10

Babylon 8
badger 115
baklavah 67, 109, 119
Baldwin of Flanders 29
Balkan Peninsula 7, 10, 44, 45
ballet 86
banking **45**, 47, 53
barbarians 23, 27, 28
barite 51, 116

barley 49, 116
baroque **83**
basketball 64, 119
bas-relief **87**
bathhouses 96
Battle of Manzikert 120
Bayar, Celal 121
bazaars **19**, 55, 96, 98
beaches **12**, 19, 52, 53, 92, 96, 98, 99, 100, 116
beans 49, 116
Bektashi Dervishes 122
Bergama 97
Beyoglu **20**, 29, 55, 117
Bible 8, 72, 98, 107, 108, 109
biomedicine 66, 117
birds 115
Black Sea 8, 17, 18, 19, 37, 99, **100**, **101**, 114, 115, 118
Black Sea Economic Cooperation Group 114
Black Sea Mountains 103
Black Stone, see Ka'bah
Blue Mosque **80**
boar 115
boating 96, 100
Bodrum **40**, **92**
book binding 91, 118
bookmaking 97
boron salts 51, 116
Bosnia 49
Bosporus 15, **16**, 18, 19, **20**, 22, 31, 83, 114
bridges **20**, 37
brown bear 115
Bucephalus **23**
Bukhara 10
Bulgaria 8, 39, 44, 114
Bulgars 28
Bursa 59, 114, 115
buses 116
business 48
bustard 115
Byzantine Empire 11, 13, 29, 31
Byzantines 12, 27, 33, 81, 82, 86, 89, 97, 100, 101, 102, 107, 109, 120, 122
Byzantium 21, 22, 23, 24, 25, 95, 117, 119
Byzas 22

Caesars 24
caliph 72
caliphate 39, 120
calligraphy 91, 118
Cankiri 104
capital, see Ankara
Cappadocia **5, 91, 104, 105**
caravanseries **11**, 81
carpet farm **90**
carpets 81, **89, 90**, 103, 106, 107, 118
castles 19, **29,** 101, 104
Caucasians 113
Celsus **82**
cement 51, 116
Central Anatolian Plateau 103, 115
Central Powers 37, 39
cereals 49, 116
chariot races 26
Charles V 34
Chechnya 121
chemical industries 51, 96, 116
cherries 101
chickpeas 49, 116
Christianity 69, 121
Christians 24, **25,** 28, 33, 34, 41, 55,
    70, 82, **97,** 98, 100, 101, 102, **105,**
    106, 113, 122
chromium 51, 116
Chrysostom, John 27
churches 26, 27, 28, 33, 98, 102,
    119, 122
Cilician plain 97, 98
Ciller, Tansu 63, 121
cinema 66, 84, 87, 117
citadel 105, 106, 109
citrus fruits 50
cliffs   6
climate 46, 115
clothing 51, **54, 61,** 116, 118
coal **50,** 51
coastline 50, 64, 96, 98, 99, 114, 116
copper 116
coffee 49, 67, 96, 116, 119
Commonwealth of Independent
    States 44
communication 116
Communists 47, 120
Comneni Dynasty 102
concubines 61, 82
Constantine I, the Great 24, **25,** 26,
    27, 119, 121
Constantine XI Paleologus,
    Emperor 31, 120

Constantinople 12, 13, **14,** 21, 24,
    25, 27, 28, **29, 30,** 31, 81, 101, 117,
    119, 120, 121, 122
constitution **37,** 39, 42, 48, 49, 61, 121
Constitutional Court 43, 113
construction 51, 53
cooking 40, **67,** 81
copper 51
cotton 49, 96, 116
cotton oil 50, 116
Council of Ministers 42
court system 43
crafts **91,** 118
crescent **30**
crops 49, 116
crude oil 51, 116
crusaders 28, **29,** 101, 120
culture 53, 81, 117, 118
Cyprus 120, 121

Dalyan River **4**
dams 50
dancing **63,** 64, **84,** 85, 86, 118
Danube 24
Dardanelles 17, 18, 114
Darius, King 18, 119
Delacroix **29**
Delphi 22
democracy 110, 111
Democratic Party 120, 121
desserts 66, 67, 119
dilber dudagi 67
Diocletian 24, 25
Diogenes 101
divorce 118
Dogubuyazit 107, 108
dolma 66
Dolmabahce Palace 82, **83**
ducks 115

early civilizations 7, 8, 9
earthquake 115, 120
Eastern Highlands 114, 115
Eastern Roman Empire, see
    Byzantine Empire
ecology 66, 117
Economic Cooperation
    Organization 114
economy 28, 39, 44, 45, 46, 47, 48,
    49, 53, 59, 79, 95, 110, 115, 116
Edirne 82, **85**
education 48, 53, 61, 64, 65, 66, 117,
    118

egalitarianism 41, 60
eggplant 66, 116, 118, 119
eggs 50, 116
Egypt 73, 94
Elazig **50**
elections 42, **110,** 118, 120, 121
electricity 116
electronics 51, 116, 117
embroidering **47,** 91, 118
energy sources 46
engineering 66, 96, 110
English **56,** 66
entertainment 53
Ephesus **52, 82,** 97
Erbakan, Necmettan 121
Ertugul, Muksin 87, 121
Erzincan 120
Erzurum 107
ethnic groups 113
ethnographic museums 109
eunuchs 33, 34
Euphrates River **7,** 103, 109, 115
exports 51, 117
Eyup Mosque 33

fabrics 51, 116
Fatih Mosque 33
family 60, 61, 62, 79
farming 55, 57, **107**
farmland 101, 115
fasting 78, 79
Fatimah 72
fencing 64, 119
Festival of Music and the Arts 95
figs 50, 96, 116
filigree art 91, 118
fishing **4,** 50, 53, 101, 116
fisheries 50, 116
fishermen **21**
Five Pillars of Islam 76, **77,** 78, 79
five-year devlopment plans 48
flag 113
Flemish 90
flowers 100
flute **80**
folk dancing **63,** 64, 118
folk music 64, 86, 118
food **40,** 66, **67,** 118, 119
football 64, 119
foreign affairs 37, 42, 47
forest products 51
forests 46, 51, 105, 115
fossil fuels 51

Fourth Crusade 28, 120
France 10, 38, 39, 117, 120
frescoes 102
fruits 116, 117
fundamentalist Muslims 44, 45, 79
furniture 51, 82, 109, 116, 117
Fuzuli 121

Galata 29
Galata Bridge 20
Galatasaray 64
Gallienus, Emperor 23, 119
Gauls 24, 58
Gaziantep 109, 114
General Agreement on Tariffs and
    Trade 114
Genesis 109
Genoese 28, 29, 31
geography 114
Georgia 8, 114
Germany 37, 39, 90, 117, 120
Ghiordes 90
Giresun 101
girls **62**, 116
gold 91, 101
Golden Fleece 18
Golden Horn **18**, 19, 20, 29, 31, 33,
    37
Gordian knot 104
Gordion 104
Goreme **105**; see also Cappadocia
government 42, 43, 44, 49, 59, 63,
    83, 113, 116, 117, 118, 119, 120
Grand Bazaar **19**, 55
Grand National Assembly 42, **43**,
    113
granite 51, 116
grapes 50, **96**, 105, 109, 116
Great Britain 24, 38, 39, 120
Great Flood 108
Great Plague 28
Greece 8, 38, 39, 44, 95, 96, 114, 120
Greek mythology **18**
Greek ruins **52, 86, 82, 87, 99**
Greeks 18, 19, 22, 23, 25, 29, 32, 52,
    57, 58, 85, 86, 87, 99, 101, 113,
    119, 120, 121
grotto 98
guerrillas 57, **111**, 119
gulets **40**

Haci Bektas Veli 122
Hadrian's Temple **52**

Hagia Sophia **26**, **27**, 119
Hajj 79
handball 119
hard coal 116
hare 115
harem 32, 33, 35
Harran 97, 109
Hatay Museum 98
Hattusas 103
hazelnuts 50, 100, 116
health 66, 117
hegira 71
Hellespont, see Dardanelles
Higher Education Council 65
high schools, see *lycées*
Hippodrome **26**, 36, 120
Hisarlik 22
Hittites **9**, 94, 97, **103**
Holbein, Hans 90
holidays 117
Holy Land 28
Holy Roman Empire 34
Homer **22**
horses 5, 26, 119
hospitals 106, 117
hotels 20, 52, 53, 65
housing 20, **58**, **59**, 60, **92**, 118
Hungary 34, 82, 122
Huns **10**
hunting 35, 53, 116
hydroelectricity 46, 53, 115

ice cream **54**
Iconium, see Konya
icons 101
Igdir 107, 108
Ilgaz 105, 116
imam 66, 77
imambayildi 66, 119
imports 48, 117
Indian Ocean 34, 122
industry 20, 48, 50, 51, 53, 59, 60,
    95, 115, 116
infanticide 76
infant mortality 117
inheritance rights 62
Inonu, Ismet 41, **42**, 122
International Children's Festival 95
International Festival 86
Iran 8, 9, 12, 44, 57, 72, 73, 107, 114,
    119
Iraq **7**, 8, 57, 114, 115, 119, 121
iron 51, 103, 116, 117

Iskederun 97
Islam 10, 11, 16, 20, 27, 30, 33, 44,
    55, **56**, **61**, **62**, **68**, 69, **70**, 71, 72,
    73, 74-79, 84, 85, 87, 89, 91, 101,
    106, 113, 114, 117-120
Islambol 16
Islamic fundamentalism 91, 110
Israel 44
Istanbul 8, 9, 12, 14-22, 27, 32, 34,
    36, 37, 38, **40**, **45**, 55, 57, **59**, 64,
    75, **80**, 81, 82, 86-89, 93, 95, 114,
    116-122
Istanbul State Opera 86
Istanbul University **65**
Italians 28, 58
Italo-Mediterranean people 58
Italy 24, 39, 117
Izmir 55, 59, **67**, 88, 95, 96, 114, 116

Janissaries 34, 36, 82, 120
January 24 Decisions 49
Jason and the Argonauts 18
Jerusalem 28, 69
Jesus 69, 73, 74, 88
jewelry 82, 91, 117, 118
Jews 55, 57, 58, 70, 113
jihad 75
journalists 62, 118
Judaism 69
Judeo Christian traditions 69, 72
judo 64, 119
Julius Caesar 106
Justinian I, Emperor 26, 27, 28,
    109, 122

Kaaba, see Ka'bah
Ka'bah **68**, 70, 71, **78**, 79
kadin gobegi 67
karate 64, 119
Kariye Byzantine Church **88**
Kars 91, 107
Kasadasi 52
Kas **99**
Kastamonu 100
Kayseri **102**
Kemal, Mustafa Pasha "Ataturk"
    16, 37, **38**, **41**, 42, 43, 45, 60, 89,
    95, 111, 120, 121, 122
Khadijah 71, 72
Khalil Mosque **108**
kilims 107
Kirkuk 121
Kirsehir 91

Kizil Irmak 115
Konrad, Suna 122
Konya 59, 91, 106
Koran, see Qur'an
Koroglu Mountains 100
Koycegiz **58**
Kucuk Ayasofya 28
Kula 90
Kurdish people 43, 56, **57**, **58**, 110, **111**, 113, 119, 120, 121
Kurdistan 58

lace 47
Ladik 91
lakes 50, 102, 105, 109, 115
Lake Tuz 114, 115
Lake Van **109**, 115
lamb **67**, 118, 119
language 56, 57, **78**
Latin 25, 56, 113, 120
leather goods 51, 116
legislative house **43**, 113
lentils 49, 116
leopards 115
Library of Celsus **82**
licorice trees 115
life expectancy 117
lignite 51, 116
Lion Gate **9**
literacy 117
literature 84, 85, 86
livestock 50, 116
lokum 67
Lucullus 101
lycées 64
lynx 115

Macedonia 22, 23, 58, 94, 98
magnesite 51, 116
Mahmoud II, Sultan **36**
maize 49, **107**, 116
manganese 51, 116
manufacturing 116
marble 51, 116
marine sciences 66, 117
marriage 79, 118
Mecca **68**, 70, 71, 72, **77**, **78**, 79
medical schools 12
medicine 59, 106
Medina 71
Mediterranean Sea 7, 8, 9, 17, 46, **92**, 96, 98, 114, 115
Mediterranean-Turkic people 58

Mehmet II, Sultan **13**, 31, 32, 81, 120, 122
Mersin 97, 116
Mesnevi 122
Mesopotamia 7, 8
Mevlana Rurni 106, 122
Mevlid Halil 109
Michael VIII Paleologus, Emperor 29, 120
Middle East Technical University **56**
Milas 91
Miletus 97, 101
military 121
milk 50, 116
Mimar Sinan University 87
minarets 5, **18**, **30**, **74**, **75**, 77
mineral resources 51
miniature painting 91, 118
mining 50, 51, 116
mohair wool 116
Mohammed II, see Fatih Mehmet II
monasteries **100**
money 114
Mongolia 10
Mongol peoples 58, 59, 106
monks 84, 85, 118
monuments 26, 53, 83, 97, 100, 106, 116
Morocco 34, 122
mosaics 33, 82, **88**, 98
Moses 73, 74
mosques 11, **17**, **18**, 20, **27**, 33, 73, 74, **75**, 76, 77, 81, 82, 98, **101**, 104, 107, **108**, 109, 119, 122
Motherland Party 113, 122
mother-of-pearl **83**
motor vehicles 116, 117
mountaineering 64, 116
Mount Ararat **8**, 9, 107, 108, 115
Mount Erciyes **102**, 105
Mount Hasan 105
Mozart, Wolfgang Amadeus 86
muezzin 75, 77
Muhammad 10, **68**, 69, **70**, 71, 72, 73, 74, 75, 76, 119
museums 83, 88, 89, 95, 98, 101, 105, 106, 109, 117, 118
music 64, **80**, 84, **85**, 86, 87, 118, 119
Muslims 32, 41, 55, 69, 71, 73, 75, **77**, **78**, 79, 84, 106, 110
mythology 18

National Democracy Party 113
natural resources 64
Nemrut Dagi **108**
New Rome 119
newspapers 116
nickel 51, 116
Nineveh 8
Noah 8, 74, 108
Noah's Pudding 108
nomads 10, 70
North Africa 122
North Atlantic Treaty Organization 114

obelisks 84
Oguz 11
oil 48, 49, 50, 51
olive oil 50, 66, 67, 116
olives **67**, 109, 115
opera 86, 95
opium poppies 116
Oracle of Delphi 22
orchestras 87, 95
Organization for Economic Coop- eration and Development 114
Orient Express 37
otter 115
Ottoman Empire 15, 37, 39, 44, 45, 81, **83**, 113, 120
Ottoman Turks 11, 13, 28-32, 34, 36, 37, 38, 56, 61, 66, 73, 74, 81, 82, 83, 87, 91, 92, 102, 104-107, 122
Ozal, Turgut 122

painting 87, 88, 90
Painting and Sculpture Museum 89, 118
palace 33, 81, 83, 105
Pamukkale 52, 106
Paris 87
parks 20
parliament 36, **37**, 42, **43**, 113
Partiya Karkeran Kurdistan 121
Pasha, Anwar 122
Pasha, Ziya 122
pastries 66, 67
peanut oil 50, 116
Peloponnese islands 32
Pergamum, see Bergama
Persian Empire 18, 19
Persian Gulf 46, 121
Persians 12, 23, 28, 56, 58, 84, 86, 89, 91, 95, 106, 119

petrochemical industry 51, 116
petroleum 46, 116, 117
Philip of Macedonia **22**, 23
Phrygians 94, 104
physicians 117
pigeons 115
pilaf 66, 118
pilgrimage, see *Hajj*
pilgrims 68
pistachio nuts 109
poetry 84, 85
poets 22, 84, 121, 122
political parties 43, 113
politics 62, 63, 79, 110, 118
polygamy 61, 62
Pontic Mountains 115
popular music 87
population 59, 60, 114
ports 9, 95, 100, 101, 116
poultry 50, 116
prayer 76, **77**, 90, 107, 118
prayer rugs 90, 107, 118
prehistoric times 22
president 42, 113
prime minister 42, 63, 113, 121,
    122
prophets 69, **70**, 74, 76

Qur'an **56**, 72, **73**, **78**
radio 116
railroads 51, 85, 116
raki 67, 119
Ramadan 78, 79
refugees **57**
religion 12, 55, 56, 69, 70, 79, 110
religious freedom 41, 113, 121
religious monarchy, see caliphate
religious sects 122
resorts 96, 99, 116
resources 48
restaurants 53, 106
rice 118, 119
rivers 50, 102, 114, 115
roads 46, 51, 116
Roman Empire 23, 24, **25**, 119
Romans 22, 23, 25, 81, 98, 94, 97,
    101, 105, 106, **108**, 119, 121
Rome 15, 23, 24, 25, 28
Roxelane 82
ruins 52, **82**, **86**, **87**, **99**, 109
Russia 18, 37, 44, 57, 107, 117, 119,
    121
Russians 28, 82, 107

Safranbolu 99
Saint Bacchus 28
Saint Helena 25
Saint Paul the Apostle 97
Saint Peter the Apostle 98
Saint Sergius 28
Saint Sophia, see Hagia Sophia
Salonika islands 32
Samarkand 10, **11**
samovars 67
samsa 119
Samsun 116
Sanliurfa **108**, 109
Satan 74
Saudi Arabia 70, 79, 117
schools 10, 12, 55, **56**, **62**, 64, 65, 66,
    106, 107
sciences 36, 48, **56**, 65, 66, 117
Scythians 18
seafood 66, 119
Sea of Marmara **17**, 19, 114
seaports 12, 46
Seleucids 98
Selim II **35**, **36**
Seljuk (town) **25**
Seljuk Empire 11, 12
Seljuk Turks 11, 12, 81, 89, 91, 95,
    104, 105, 106, 107, 109, 120
Sephardic Spanish 57
Septimus Severus, Emperor 23, 119
seraglio, see harem
service industries 53, 60, 116
Sesamos, see Amasra
Seydisehir **110**
Seyfettin, Omer 122
Seyh Galib 121
Shiite Muslims 55, 72
shipping 101
shipyard **40**
silk rugs **89**
silkworms 116
Sinan, Mimar **75**, 82, 87, 104, 105,
    107, 122
Sinasi 122
Sinop 100, 101
Sivas 106
skiing 64, 102, 116, 107, 119
slavery 61, 75, 76, 118
Smyrna 95
snakes 115
soccer, see football
Social Democratic Populist Party
    113

social relations 61, 62
social service 75
soil erosion 115
solar energy 66, 117
Soviet Union 8, 44, 120
Spain 34, 58, 73
Spanish 57
Sparta 23
spas 52, 102, 116
spice market **40**
sports 63, 64, 119
stadium 99
stained glass 118
Stamboul **19**, 20, 117
statism 47
statues 26, 33
steel 51, 116, 117
Sufi mystic 106, 118
sugar beets 49, 116
Suleymaniye Mosque **75**, 82, 122
Suleyman the Magnificent **34**, **35**
Sultanahmet Mosque **17**
sultans 31, 33, 35, 36, 37, 61, 120,
    122
Sumer 7
Sumerians 109
sunflowers **50**, **104**
sunflower-seed oil 50, 116
sunken city 99
Sunni Muslims 55, 72, 113
sutlac 67
swimming 64
Syria 8, 57, 97, 109, 114

table tennis 64, 119
Tahir, Kemal 122
Tarsus 97
Taurus Mountains 97, 103, 115
taxes 77
taxis 116
tea **49**, 67, 96, 100, 119
tea leaves 49, 116
technical training 45, 48, 64, 65,
    117
telephone 116
television 66, 87, 116, 117, 121
temple 68, 70
tennis 64
terraced land **49**, **96**
terrorism 49, 110
textiles 96, 98, 117
theater 84, 85, 86, 95, 96
Theodosius II, Emperor 27, 119

thorium 51, 116
Thracian 94
Tigris River **7,** 46, 103, 109, 115
tobacco 49, 51, 96, 100, 116
Tokat 106
tombs 82, 95, 105
Topkapi Palace **32,** **33,** 35, 81, **83,** 86, 117
topography 8, 114
tourism 52, 53, 65, 97, 99, 116
Trabzon **100,** 101, **110**
trade 58, 96, 117
transportation 53, 116
Trebizond, see Trabzon
Troy 22, 97
True Path Party 113, 121
tufa **105**
tungsten 51, 116
Tunisia 82, 120
Turkic peoples 9, 10, 11
Turkish Airlines 116
Turkish and Islamic Art Museum 89, 117
Turkish Republic 16, 42, 44, 45, 113, 120
Turkish Riviera 98, **99,** 116
Uludare **57**
Ulus 95
United Kingdom 117

United Nations 114, 120, 121
United States 39, 114, 117, 120, 121
universities 64, **65,** 66, 87, 117, 120
University of Ankara 87
University of Istanbul 120
Upper Mesopotamian Plain 108, 109
Ur 8
Urfa, see Sanliurfa
Urgup **54**
Usak 91
Uskudar 20, 21, 22, 117, 119
Uzbek **11**
Uzbekistan 10, **11**

Van Eyck, Jan 90
vegetable oils 50, 116
vegetables 66, 96, 116, 119
Virgil 22
volcano **102**
volleyball 64, 119

War of Independence **38,** 95, **108,** 120
water 14, 21
water pipe **60**
water sports 100
water-supply system 37

weaving 89, 90, 118
weight lifting 64, 119
wheat 49, 116
whirling dervishes **84,** 85, 106, 118, 122
whitewater rafting 53, 64, 102, 116
wildlife 115
wine 67, 119
women 47, **54, 56, 60, 61,** 62, 63, 71, 110, 118
women's rights 60
wood engraving 91, 100, 118
wool 50, 116
World War I 37, 38, 39, 45, 48, 120, 122
World War II 48
wrestling 64, 119

Xerxes 19
yachting 64, 119
Yiddish 58
yogurt 118
Young Turk Movement 37, 41, 42, 120, 122
youth groups 63, 64, 118
Yugoslavia 45

zakat 77
Zile 106

About the Author

Luis Baralt was born and raised in Cuba but has lived most of his adult life in such places as New York, Ottawa, Chicago, Mexico City, and various European cities. His University of Havana education trained him for the diplomatic service, but he later switched to other pursuits when political developments in Cuba prompted him to resign his diplomatic post in Canada.

He then became editor of Encyclopaedia Britannica's foreign-language publications, including *Enciclopedia Barsa,* a 15-volume set based on the EB and directed at young Hispanic and Latin American readers. He has since been editor and/or managing director of various publishing ventures. He is the author of two collections of short stories.

Mr. Baralt and his wife Ariane, who is from Holland, presently live in Spain and travel widely with their three children, based in places as far removed from each other as Chicago, San Ramon (Costa Rica), and Bangkok (Thailand).